Reflections & Recipes OF CHEF JUDI

JUDI GALLAGHER

AuthorHouse™
1663 Liberty Drive
Bloomington, IN 47403
www.authorhouse.com
Phone: 1 (800) 839-8640

Published by AuthorHouse 06/20/2018

ISBN: 978-1-5462-4211-6 (sc)
ISBN: 978-1-5462-4212-3 (e)

Library of Congress Control Number: 2018905796

Print information available on the last page.

DEDICATION

. . . .

This book is dedicated to the loving and mighty Pauline Kopper.
It was and always will be her undying fortitude and soulful cooking spirit that serve as my guideposts in life.
My Nana: all five feet of integrity, courage, and love of family.
Because of you, I will always take the ripest tomato, the fluffiest of matzo balls and the crispiest tart apples.
Nana, you taught me -- love of food, kindness toward all, and, never stray from humble pie.

Acknowledgement:
Mark Sickles Photography

FORWARD

....

This book is about a five year old child who lived in a home where food was everything.

She woke up smelling blueberry pancakes, bacon or sausages in the griddle pan, and the first thing she asked was, "What's for dinner tonight?" Although this picky child preferred Bumble Bee tuna sandwiches on toasted rye over cereal, she was obsessed with the colors and textures and flavors that come together in a simmering pot. And, she relished the peace that it brought.

There was something magical about the kitchen, as she found solace from difficult times. Even at a young age, planning dinner parties and playing restaurant with her Mom spelled safety.

As the youngest of three, the older siblings didn't much care for this kind of escape but her Nana, Mother and Aunt Helen ushered her into the world of cinnamon and sugar (gently mixing with sour cream for the blintze topping and sweet and sour stuffed cabbage that just made you dream of the sweet plump raisins in the sauce).

She watched Julia Child and the Galloping Gourmet and Jacques Pepin years before it was cool to be a foodie. She dreamed of donning a starched white chef coat and placing copper pans on flames, just to watch the butter melt before adding fresh filet of sole.

Somehow, her fairy princess castle would be made with large ovens and oversized mixers and coolers full of bright fresh seasonal summer tomatoes and strawberries and homemade whipped cream.

She focused on her dream, her career and a path forward when times of sadness and loss nearly broke her.

This is my story. How my connection and love affair with food healed my soul.

May these stories and recipes bring you the same comfort. JG

CONTENTS

INTRODUCTION

Writing a cookbook has been dangling in the back of my mind for many years. But, beyond recipes and visuals, how much did I want the book to reflect the obstacles, as well as the trusted mentors, met throughout the years?

For me, <u>Recipes and Reflections</u> depicts a young girl's passion for stirring, chopping, baking and eating all things delicious. It also represents the lingering pain and consistent fears that a culinary life can repair.

For all those who had been told that a restaurant kitchen was a man's place -- see us roar. And, to those supportive leaders who opened the magical door to a culinary world for me, this Chef is forever grateful. You walked me into a world that taught --- one committed to a classically-trained and passionately-protected culinary career can spark creative and healing forces: one cracked egg or one roast chicken at a time.

For all those who explore their own kitchen and farmers markets, may your culinary pathways lead to wholeness and happiness.

Chapter One

PERSPECTIVE

· ·

They say that life only gives you what can be handled.

Malarkey, too many times life seemingly lusts in kicks to the gut and daggers through the heart.

While never really wanting a second restaurant, in reality, a metaphor for not wanting a marriage that was asphyxiating me, a larger than life mother-in-law imperiously let it be known that a much more prominent, spacious restaurant was proper for her son.

With the screaming sound in my head bellowing: "Run, Run-away". the disabled sense of self succumbed. Although rich with joy and strength of purpose, for perhaps the first time in my life, by being bonded with my son, Eric, making homemade baby food, strolling the boulevard at will, relishing a year away from the 80-hours work week, so incapacitated was I that the only option was the second restaurant.

Oh, the maternal delectation continued as much as possible. Like the time I had 2 1/2 years old, Eric, join me at work, safely observing (each other) from the hallway – a hallway where nine sweet berry-bursting varieties of homemade muffins were cooling. Alas, before long, as I glanced quickly, there was Eric on his Mickey Mouse stool, availing himself of the opportunity to painstakingly stick his finger in every single muffin. Row upon row, the pineapple, coconut muffins and blueberry, crumble muffins bore a toddler's fingerprint.

Even precious instances like this, with all their wonderment, could not offset the shock of powerlessly enduring a marriage crumbling more than any muffin. There was meanness; there were anger issues. Thus, the trauma and the impotence I felt was too remnant of an abusive and mentally unstable father.

As fear grew and violence dispersed, I turned to my sister Hilary; Hilary, my long time refuge in escaping the paternal pain. A simple phone call cemented that Eric and I would move back to my childhood town and into her new two-bedroom condo: a genesis perhaps.

Confidently, Hilary assured me that with my cooking and management skills, a new path could be paved; one bereft from the near-surface rage that was being endured both at home and at the restaurant.

This was the final conversation I would have with Hilary.

While preparing an evening meal and dancing around the house with Eric, a dreaded phone call reshaped my world forever. Hilary had collapsed outside of Fenway Park, on her way to meet my brother for a late fall Red Sox vs Yankees baseball game. She had no heartbeat when the paramedics arrived. She was pronounced dead in the hospital 10 hours later.

My rock, my bestie, the inner soul, who shielded me from the rage and torment of a mentally ill father and the world that created him, was now lying at Beth Israel hospital, close enough to see the lights of Fenway Park, but without a trace of brain movement. In the most prolonged ten hours of my life, I sat and witnessed her body give way to the afterlife. So much of me was also gone, hope for a future secured by Hilary's watchful guidance dashed into mounds of unspeakable grief.

The comfort of my son's innocence and animation, as well as his dependence, kept me going. There's something about a little boy obsessively watching the Wizard of Oz, wanting to act out the parts, or hanging on my leg as I frosted cupcakes for a pre-school party, that challenges grief's emptiness.

The true kindness of customers, as well as my staff and dear friends, provided semblance of light on those starless nights. They picked me up of the floor, sometimes literally, babysat, brought meals and just sat by my side… the human touch.

A regular customer, Elliot Margolis, who owned the local sporting goods store, stopped me one day in the restaurant. As he slid his coffee to the side and ever so gently leaned over the counter, he knowingly whispered: "Death gives you perspective."

These words delivered certainty and shape for my new direction --- one of healing for me and encouragement for the young son who would need my protection.

And then, it was when I had to drive from Northern Massachusetts to both console my Mother's broken heart, and, to help her cope with the chaotic behavior of my father's near constant dance with madness, that I began to receive odd phone calls from vendors.

Checks had bounced; invoices were going unpaid. Something was amiss. BJ's in the Park, our restaurant, was going broke….and fast.

I am a person who worries about any bill….was then, am now, and, so, not owing any money, maintaining every receipt, paying in advance, at every chance, was my credo…just as Mom taught me.

However, in my deep grief, I was not able to tend to the books. In the 2-3 months since my sister's death, every single bank account was emptied, squandering our personal account and Eric's college account as well. (Guess who?)

Yes, literally, it was all gone. With about $5.00 in my wallet and with sheer terror of not being able to feed my son, pay his preschool, pay any bills -- I sat on the floor; I cried for hours.

The trance and trauma that absorbed me was not a delusion. When I was physically able…I called my Mom. Within 2 ½ hours, my Mother appeared at the front door with a full bag of deli from Rein's, a whole turkey, a platter of roast beef and stacks of steaks for the freezer and…. a plan. She hugged me, as we both cried, and she allowed me to slip back onto the floor in a near fetal position. "Judi", she eventually whispered: "I will stay all week. You can go to bed and pull the covers up. BUT, after three days you need to get up. You have a college education and the work ethic of a true pro. We can figure out your next steps; I will stock your freezer, fill your oil tank and love on Eric. REMEMBER? This is not the worst nightmare you have lived through."

On day three I got up, only knowing that I needed to cook or bake.

Borrowing cash from Mom, I set out to buy oatmeal cookie ingredients: my famous claim to fame since I was in third grade and initially answered the urge to bake. I baked and baked and baked. Then I brought some samples to local gourmet store, just about pretending to be Betty Crocker herself, and there began the new road of recovery. Through melting butter, brown sugar and rolled oats, Just Desserts was born.

In order to care for Eric as much as possible, I worked all available nighttime bartending shifts, hired a God-send, live in babysitter, and, slept intermittently for a few hours, as I arose near dawn to bake the cookies and muffins.

Eventually, early-morning space was affordable at the restaurant I worked at…with two convection ovens and a used Hobart mixer, my list of clients slowly began to grow.

I will forever be grateful for the two most reputable businesses that started my dessert company's prominence: <u>Legal Seafoods</u> and <u>DeLucas Markets</u> in Boston. <u>Just Desserts</u> grew and grew.

Within a year I had a rental space and a business partner of my own who made enviable cheesecakes. We even had a play area built for our children with, of course, Easy Bake Ovens. (The kids got the extra batter and occasionally set up shop across from the YMCA where doting women, running out of exercise class, paid them well over the quarter they were charging.) My marketing plan worked, under stock the shelves to build more demand. Boston was abuzz with <u>Just Desserts</u> cookies, chocolate mousse brownies and mini muffins.

<u>Just Desserts</u> saved me. Not just financially, but the aroma of butter and brown sugar melting into soft crispy edged cookies gave me back the passion to cook, bake, do everything I could with my hands. This time ingredients were kept simpler, as I struggled financially without any child support, I learned braising of tougher meats and multiple new pasta recipes (box pasta very inexpensive at the time) made our table at home an enjoyable respite from the darkness of betrayal.

Slowly, very slowly, I paid back my Mom, my lawyer, and, eventually realized that, even with the ceaselessness of a deranged Father, the immeasurable pain brought by the death of a 30 year old sister, and, the powerlessness and depression that was being endured from my marriage, I did have the strength to get up off the floor.

That strength was foundational. That capability was named Nana.

RECIPES

APPLE COFFEE CAKE FRENCH TOAST WITH WARM APPLE COMPOTE

Description

If you aren't serving a crowd you may have some leftover pastry. I freeze the extra pieces and make either a bread pudding or apple French toast with the remaining pieces. Perfect for a main course at brunch the coffee cake ring is so sweet and delicious by itself that you won't have to work too hard to create this dish. You may substitute fresh apricots when they are in season for the apples. Use a splash of apricot brandy or regular brandy instead of the apple brandy.

Ingredients

1 stick unsalted butter - cut into Tbsp.
1 bag Macintosh apples-peeled, cored and sliced
2 tsp. cinnamon plus 1 tsp.
1-1/2 tsp. pure vanilla extract
1 cup sugar - separated into half cups
1/4 cup Calvados (apple brandy)

1/4 cup water (if needed for apples)
1 coffee cake ring
1 jar pumpkin butter or plum butter
1 cup fresh whipped cream
4 eggs
1 cup half and half

Directions

In a medium saucepan, add apples, 1 tsp. cinnamon, 1/4 cup sugar.

Heat until apples are soft and chunky (occasionally mashing with a whisk).

Add water if needed during the cooking process. Blend in Calvados and let sit on stove without heat.

In the meantime- Slice the coffee cake on the bias.

Heat a large sauté pan and add 1 Tbsp. butter.

Whip eggs with half-and-half, 1 tsp. vanilla and 1 tsp. cinnamon.

Dip the coffee cake slices into the batter, turn to fully cover both sides and add to hot griddle or pan with melted butter.

Grill cake slices on both sides until golden brown. Add more butter to the pan as needed.

Arrange French toast slices on a platter. Brush with pumpkin or plum butter. Top with warm apple compote and a dollop of fresh whipped cream. Garnish with cinnamon and sugar.

CINNAMON BANANA STREUSEL MUFFINS

Description

From the very first Main Street Café recipe cards.

Ingredients

1 1/2 cups all-purpose flour
1 tsp. baking soda
1 tsp. baking powder
1/2 tsp. salt
1/3 cup unsalted butter room temperature
3/4 cup white sugar
1 egg
1/2 tsp. vanilla extract
3 medium bananas mashed

Cinnamon Streusel

1/3 cup all-purpose flour
2 Tbsp. brown sugar
2 Tbsp. ground cinnamon
2 Tbsp. unsalted butter room temperature

Glaze

1 cup powdered sugar
2 Tbsp. heavy cream

Directions

Preheat oven to 350 degrees °F.

Line a 12-cup muffin pan with paper liners.

In a large bowl, mix together 1 1/2 cups flour, baking soda, baking powder and salt.

In the bowl of a stand mixer, beat together sugar and butter for about 4 minutes.

Add the egg and vanilla extract, whisk until combined. Stir in the mashed bananas.

Add the wet mixture to the dry mixture and mix until just combined.

Spoon batter into prepared muffin cups.

In a small bowl, combine all-purpose flour, sugar, and cinnamon. Cut in butter until mixture is crumbly. Sprinkle evenly over muffins.

Bake for 20 - 25 minutes, until a toothpick, inserted into the center, comes out clean.

Drizzle with glaze.

GINGERSNAP COOKIES

Description

A family favorite and a New England traditional cookie recipe. Save the broken ones and freeze for garnishes and cheesecake crusts.

Ingredients

2 1/2 cups all-purpose flour
2 1/4 tsp. baking soda
1 Tbsp. ground ginger
1/2 tsp. fine sea salt
1/2 tsp. ground allspice
1/2 tsp. freshly ground white pepper
1/4 tsp. ground cinnamon

1 cup (2 sticks) unsalted butter, at room temperature
1/2 cup firmly packed dark brown sugar
1/2 cup granulated sugar
6 Tbsp. unsulfured molasses
1 large egg, at room temperature
1/2 cup sanding or granulated sugar, for rolling

Directions

In a medium bowl, whisk together the flour, baking soda, salt, ginger, allspice, pepper, and cinnamon.

In the bowl of a stand mixer fitted with the paddle attachment, beat the butter with the brown sugar and granulated sugar until light and fluffy. Use a rubber spatula to scrape down the sides of the bowl. Beat in molasses and the egg. On low speed, beat in the flour mixture until just combined. Cover and refrigerate until firm, at least 1 hour.

When ready to bake, heat the oven to 300 degrees °F. Line two rimmed baking sheets with silicone baking mats or parchment paper.

Remove the dough from refrigerator. Using a small ice cream scoop, shape the dough into 1-inch balls. Place the sanding sugar in a medium bowl and roll the cookie balls in the sugar a few at a time to completely and thoroughly coat.

Place half of the dough balls 2 inches apart on the prepared baking sheets. Using the bottom of a drinking glass, flatten the cookies until they measure about 1/4 inch thick. Bake until browned, 10 to 12 minutes. Transfer to a wire rack to cool completely.

Repeat with the remaining dough balls. Store in an airtight container for up to 2 days.

FLOURLESS CHOCOLATE TORTE

Description

Not your Easy Bake Oven recipe, this dense torte packs in the chocolate flavor.

Ingredients

1 cup semisweet or bittersweet chocolate chips
1/2 cup (8 Tbsp.) unsalted butter
3/4 cup granulated sugar
1/4 tsp. salt
1 to 2 tsp. espresso powder, optional
1 tsp. vanilla extract, optional

3 large eggs
1/2 cup unsweetened cocoa powder,
Dutch-process cocoa preferred
Glaze
1 cup semisweet or bittersweet chocolate chips
1/2 cup heavy cream

Directions

Preheat the oven to 375 degrees °F. Lightly grease a metal 8" round cake pan; cut a piece of parchment to fit, grease it, and lay it in the bottom of the pan. See "tips," below.

To make the cake:

Put the chocolate and butter in a microwave-safe bowl, and heat until the butter is melted and the chips are soft. Stir until the chips melt, reheating briefly if necessary. You can also do this over a burner set at very low heat. Transfer the melted chocolate/butter to a mixing bowl.

Stir in the sugar, salt, espresso powder, and vanilla. Espresso enhances chocolate flavor much as vanilla does; using 1 teaspoon will simply enhance the flavor, while 2 teaspoons will lend a hint of mocha to the cake.

Add the eggs, beating briefly until smooth. Add the cocoa powder and mix just to combine.

Spoon the batter into the prepared pan.

Bake the cake for 25 minutes; the top will have formed a thin crust, and it should register at least 200 degrees °F on an instant-read thermometer inserted into its center.

Remove it from the oven and cool it in the pan for 5 minutes.

Loosen the edges of the pan with a table knife or nylon spreader and turn it out onto a serving plate. The top will now be on the bottom; that's fine. Also, the edges will crumble a bit, which is also fine. Allow the cake to cool completely before glazing.

To make the glaze:

Combine the chocolate and cream in a microwave-safe bowl, and heat until the cream is very hot, but not simmering. Remove from the microwave and stir until the chocolate melts and the mixture is completely smooth.

Spoon the glaze over the cake, spreading it to drip over the sides a bit. Allow the glaze to set for several hours before serving the cake.

HUMMINGBIRD CAKE

Description

My dear friend Marsha Fottler and I have made this cake for years as a donation for a true old fashioned cake auction held every year. I often double the recipe, make a triple layer cake and there will be enough batter when you double it to have muffins in the morning as well.

Ingredients

3 cups all-purpose flour
1 tsp. baking soda
1 tsp. salt
2 cups sugar
1 tsp. ground cinnamon
3 large eggs, beaten
1 cup vegetable oil
1 1/2 tsp. vanilla extract
1 (8 oz.) cans crushed pineapple, undrained

1 cup chopped pecans
2 cups chopped bananas
1/2 cup chopped pecans
Cream Cheese Frosting
1 (8 oz.) packages cream cheese, softened
1/2 cup butter softened
1 (16 oz.) packages powdered sugar, sifted
1 tsp. pure vanilla extract

Directions

Combine flour, baking soda, salt, sugar and ground cinnamon in a large bowl.
Add eggs, and oil, stirring until dry ingredients are moistened.
(Do not beat) Stir in vanilla, pineapple, 1 cup pecans, and bananas.
Pour batter into 3 greased and floured 9" round cake pans.
Bake at 350 degrees °F for 25 to 30 minutes or until a wooden pick inserted in center comes out clean.
Cool in pans on wire racks 10 minutes; remove from pans, and cool completely on wire racks.
Spread Cream Cheese Frosting between layers and on top and sides of cake; sprinkle 1/2 cup chopped pecans on top.
Store in refrigerator.
Cream Cheese Frosting:
Beat cream cheese and butter at medium speed, with an electric mixer until smooth.
Gradually add powdered sugar, beating at low speed until light and fluffy.
Stir in vanilla.
Yield: 3 cups.

JORDAN MARSH BLUEBERRY MUFFINS

Description

Needless to say, this recipe was the ultimate score for my Mom's best friend, Cynthia Krozen.

Ingredients

1/2 cup softened butter
1 1/4 cups sugar
2 eggs
1 tsp. vanilla extract
2 cups flour
1/2 tsp. salt
2 tsp. baking powder
1/2 cup milk
2 cups blueberries, washed, drained and picked over
3 tsp. sugar

Directions

Preheat the oven to 375 degrees °F.

Cream the butter and 1 1/4 cups sugar until light.

Add the eggs, one at a time, beating well after each addition. Add vanilla.

Sift together the flour, salt and baking powder, and add to the creamed mixture alternately with the milk.

Crush 1/2 cup blueberries with a fork and mix into the batter. Fold in the remaining whole berries.

Line a 12 cup standard muffin tin with cupcake liners, and fill with batter. Sprinkle the 3 tsp. sugar over the tops of the muffins and bake at 375 degrees °F for about 30-35 minutes.

Remove muffins from tin and cool at least 30 minutes. Store, uncovered, or the muffins will be too moist the second day, if they last that long.

Note:

You can top with crumbled brown sugar, chopped pecans and brown sugar if you prefer a streusel topping.

The recipe is so versatile. To make banana muffins simply mash three ripe bananas instead of the blueberries and 2 tsp. cinnamon to the batter.

AMARETTO OLIVE OIL CAKE

Description

Olive Oil Cake' Don't knock it till you try it. A moist cake just waiting for a little Amaretto whipped cream for the top.

Ingredients

3 large eggs
1 cup granulated sugar
1 1/2 cups whole milk
1 cup extra-virgin olive oil, plus more for coating the pan
1/4 cup amaretto liqueur
1 Tbsp. finely grated orange zest

1 1/2 cups all-purpose flour, plus more for dusting the pan
1/2 cup coarse-ground cornmeal
1/2 tsp. baking powder
1/2 tsp. baking soda
Pinch of salt
Powdered sugar, for garnish

Directions

Heat the oven to 350 degrees °F and arrange a rack in the middle.

Coat a 9-inch round cake pan with olive oil and flour; tap out the excess.

In a large bowl, whisk together eggs and granulated sugar until well blended and light in color.

Add milk, olive oil, amaretto, and orange zest and mix well.

In another bowl, stir together flour, cornmeal, baking powder, baking soda, and salt.

Add egg mixture to the dry ingredients, stirring until just blended (the batter will be slightly lumpy; do not overmix).

Pour the batter into the prepared cake pan.

Bake until a toothpick inserted into the center of the cake comes out with only a few crumbs, about 40 to 50 minutes.

Remove from the oven and place on a wire rack to cool completely.

When the cake has cooled, run a knife around the perimeter of the pan and invert the cake onto a serving plate.

Dust with powdered sugar, cut into 12 pieces, and serve.

STRAWBERRIES ROMANOFF

Description

An all-time favorite 1960's classic, I prefer to serve mine with a sliced shortcake biscuit to the side or scone to ensure every drop.

Ingredients

2 pt. strawberries, washed and stemmed

1/4 cup sugar

1/4 cup orange liqueur, such as
Grand Marnier or Cointreau

1 pt. vanilla ice cream (I prefer Haagen
Dazs for the rich fat content)

1 cup heavy cream

2 Tbsp. zest of orange

6-8 whole berries

Buttermilk shortcake biscuits

Directions

Slice the strawberries.

In a large bowl, toss three-quarters of them with the sugar and orange liqueur.

Refrigerate at least 1 hour to macerate.

Put the ice cream in the refrigerator to soften.

Place the cream and half the macerated strawberries in a cold mixing bowl.

With an electric mixer, whip to soft peaks, about 12 minutes.

Fold in the ice cream.

Distribute the cream among 6 tall martini glasses.

Mix the plain sliced berries with the remaining macerated berries and place on top of the cream.

Garnish with a whole berry - stem on and zest of orange.

CRANBERRY CHUTNEY

Description

Not just for Thanksgiving any more, I love making chutneys to share as a hostess gift or alongside any poultry.

Ingredients

1/2 cup Spanish Onions, small dice
1 Tbsp. ginger, minced
1 orange, zested & juiced
1 cup sugar

1 cup white vinegar
2 cinnamon sticks
12 oz. package cranberries

Directions

In a saucepan, combine the onions, ginger, orange juice and zest, sugar, vinegar and cinnamon sticks.
Bring to a boil and cook down to a syrup (about 15 minutes).
Add cranberries and continue to cook until the cranberries have all "popped".
Cool slightly. Place in mason jars.

Chapter Two

NANA-STRENGTH PERSONIFIED

I wonder just how or when one's childhood infatuations so powerfully influence who she will become. How one's drive of hard work gets deeply rooted, where one's resilience and grit becomes rock solidly embedded, and, just how one's, securely fastened, social identity gets formed. Pretty heavy questions, for sure. For me, pretty clear answers, by age six.

By then, I had begun absorbing everything my Nana did with her hands in a kitchen. Sacred rituals were born. From tying on her apron to rolling matzo balls, to frying golden crispy shreds of potatoes and onions. Pauline Kopper was one part defiant, one part intellectual with a flaming liberal bent, and, one part seeped in the Jewish tradition.

Having to drop out of school age 13 to support her family, yet made an investment of a lifetime in AT&T (where she worked for many years) Nana spoke fluent Yiddish and Hungarian and, even at 4 feet 11 inches tall, had the gumption, to tell the kosher butcher that he hadn't cut the brisket properly last week.

Standing in her tiny Yonkers kitchen, where we, her grandchildren, would securely serve as loyal assistants, the experience was much more than a culinary one. The bonding was an enterprise in lifelong learning. Whether it was giving me a piggy back ride around her one bedroom apartment (though I was getting much taller than she) or helping to line up Scrabble pegs in order to strategically create a sensational domino effect, Nana was my idol.

She schlepped me to numerous stores each day to gather the dinner's ingredients, sometimes twelve blocks away from one another, because the store in between was run by a felon or *that* produce man charged six cents more for a tomato, or quite simply that store didn't have the perfect ingredients! She doted on me with a lunch at the automat, and a strawberry ice cream sundae in a cup, even though I couldn't take another bite. She further insisted on a pastry or cookies an hour later and then while she began to wrap her apron around that little waist of hers, she would fetch a ½ sour pickle to 'tie me over', while performing her cooking magic. She prepared fast but precise, trimming and saving every extra little item in colored casserole dishes that seemed, oh, so precious and beautiful. I learned much later that those dishes held the valuable scraps that would perfectly pronounce a later snack, appetizer, or, meal......a dab of tuna fish, some cracker bits, or, an olive for proper garnish.

The creation of meals truly was a symphony and Nana's love for culture (and later mine) did not end there. On many, many occasions, together, walking arm in arm, we would attend a movie or the Rockettes show; dancing back to the apartment and, of course, stopping at the corner candy store for a round tin of cherry sour drops, my favorite.

Yes, Nana was THE conductor in the kitchen: whether chopping a full head of cabbage, like a professional Japanese sumo or, cleaning a turkey carcass after Thanksgiving, like there was a bus load of hungry people waiting for the three meals she could prepare with those leftovers.

Nana was disciplined, keeping kosher in respect to what she ate, as well as keeping dairy and meat separated at home. However, when she came to our house she ate almost everything...but in small portions. Her only refusal was that she never ever had a McDonald's hamburger or any other fast-food hamburger. My little perfectionist made only homemade hamburgers with thick slices of onion.

I cannot count the amount of times my sister and I begged her to try a McDonald's, but, as a child of an orthodox rabbi and strict, distant, cold mother, even at age of 75 she would not break that kosher law. Disciplined...meticulous... creative...downright rugged: for she was the offspring of complicated and stern parents and grandparents who withstood paucity and foresaw Hitler's Eastern Europe by fleeing to the United States.

This lovely little blue eyed kitchen wizard, who made three homemade soups each day for her children's lunch, and took immeasurable pride in the uniqueness of her sour cream coffee cake, scrumptious brisket, succulent roast chicken and homemade horseradish sauce never ever taught her daughter nor her sons anything about a kitchen, Nana's castle. That is, except me...her youngest and most vulnerable grandchild.

I inherited the stamina and willful hands to dive into bowls of flour and sugar or spoons with chicken fat dripping, while simultaneously stirring something braising on the back burner.

Nana had the smoothest tanned skin, no doubt originating from daily schleps to buy her ingredients, as well as the medicinal result from a daily piece of toast with a little dab of schmaltz.

Although air conditioning and spicy foods gave her problems, she would never complain, even when power-walking to regular Radio City Music Hall productions, like Yul Brynner in *The Kind and I*. Interestingly, post production was frequently followed by a visit from my odd, but kind, Uncle Jonas, whom we always met at a specific diner where the desserts swirled around a clear refrigerator case and the hostess, with big black hair, sat on a stool.

Uncle Jonas wore big political buttons, and ate quickly. His usual was a bowl of beef and barley soup, followed by stuffed cabbage, mashed potatoes and tapioca pudding. He always gave me a quarter after showing me a few coin tricks. Then, off he went, dabbing his perspiring forehead and shaking hands with various people sitting in booths reading newspapers and talking about the days' events.

Jonas was actually a genius. Literally, the man that had one of the highest IQ's in the state of New York, but somehow never fit into society just right. Nana, his mother, doted on him, always paying the check, while slipping some bills in his pocket...though she thought I didn't notice due to preoccupation with my strawberry cake.

Nana had this knack for *knowing*: Jonas' need for nurturanc*e,* my older sister's craving for chocolate, my big brother's desire for large portions, my mother's yearning for safety, even my unstable father's obsessions. Nana knew her power.

As one would expect from our intimacy, Nana and I talked about greater things other than food. She taught me politics... strong political perspectives... as well empathy for those less fortunate...unswerving compassion for those in any need. She beckoned that to volunteer was the true way to grow as a person...and that 'to give of oneself' was a non negotiable.

A college education? This titan with an eighth grade education had dreams for her grandchildren, hatched, no doubt, as she rolled buttered layers of nuts and honey and flaky pastry. She somehow first scraped and then invested and saved and saved for each one of us to fulfill her vision of a college education. And, It wasn't until I opened my first restaurant and found my Nana outside on a bench with tears rolling down her face that I understood my true apprenticeship, acknowledged my trusted mentor, recognized my faithful hero.

Concerned that she was crying, I asked her if she liked my restaurant, she simply smiled at me, conveniently pinched my cheek, and, whispered in that soft but secure voice: "You made me so proud".

This little, not quite 5 foot, lady gave me much more than a culinary destiny or my career path. She filled my generous heart with an unyielding constitution and an unbending fortitude. She also crafted a healing soul for all things delicious and homemade.

RECIPES

PAULINE KOPPER'S FAMILY NON-DAIRY NOODLE PUDDING

Description

My Nana won a trip to the Catskills with this recipe. To this day it is a Sunday favorite with roast chicken.

Ingredients

1/2 lb. egg noodles
2 eggs scrambled
1/4 cup sugar
3 Tbsp. orange juice
1 tsp. pure vanilla extract
1 medium apple, peeled and shredded

1 cup raisins
1/4 cup Crisco
Cinnamon
Approximately 2-3 handfuls crushed cornflakes (the cornflakes are a binder so feel for the consistency)

Directions

Boil noodles as directed.
Combine eggs with sugar and cinnamon and beat well.
Add orange juice and vanilla and grated apple.
Stir into cooked noodles. Melt ¼ cup of Crisco in a large pan. Pour off 2 Tbsp. into noodle mixture.
Mash cornflakes and add one handful at a time. Pour noodle pudding into fry pan. Brown about 10 minutes on medium high heat. Cover pan with a large plate and flip over. Slide noodle pudding back into pan and brown other side.

VEGETABLE LATKES

Description

Hanukkah, the festival of Lights Celebrates bringing families and friends together to enjoy latkes; fried potatoes to symbolize the miracle of one can of oil lasting 8 nights. Since I make latkes several nights during the holiday, I like to mix up the ingredients.

Ingredients

1 zucchini, grated
1 yellow squash, grated
1 1/2 tsp. kosher salt, divided
1 tsp. canola oil
1 small leek, sliced
1 large baking potato, peeled
1/2 sweet potato, peeled
1/4 tsp. black pepper
1/2 small red onion, minced

3 Tbsp. all-purpose flour
2 Tbsp. matzo meal
1 large egg, beaten
1/2 tsp. baking soda
1/2 tsp. garlic salt
1/4 tsp. hot sauce
Canola oil
Sour cream
Caviar (optional)

Directions

Arrange grated zucchini and squash on a large baking pan; sprinkle with 1 teaspoon kosher salt.
Let vegetables rest 15 minutes.
Drain well, pressing between paper towels, and set aside.
Heat 1 tsp. canola oil in a small sauté pan, and sauté leek 3 minutes or until soft; set aside.
Grate potatoes and press between paper towels to remove excess water.
Place potatoes in a large bowl; add zucchini, squash, leek, remaining 1/2 tsp. salt, and 1/4 tsp. white pepper, and stir gently.
Add red onion and next 6 ingredients, stirring gently to combine.
Heat 2 to 4 tablespoons oil in a large nonstick skillet over medium-high heat.
Spoon heaping Tbsp. of latke mixture, if you have one use a scoop, squeeze out extra liquid, and form into flat patties.
Fry latkes, in batches, 1 to 1 1/2 minutes on each side or until golden.
Remove from skillet and drain on paper towels.
Top each with a piece of smoked salmon, a dollop of sour cream, and caviar.
Serve immediately.

BAVARIAN CREAM

Description

My Mother used to make cream cakes and all I ever wanted was a big scoop of Bavarian cream. While some recipes call for instant pudding, it is so much better to make it a classic French style.

You can use puff pastry or baked tart shell.

Ingredients

4 cups of heavy whipping cream
1 vanilla bean sliced in half long ways
6 egg yolks
1/2 cup of sugar
5 oz. of cold water
1/4 oz. of gelatin

Directions

Whisk 2 cups of heavy whipping cream in a standing mixer with the whisk attachment on high speed until stiff peaks are formed and then cool.

In a medium bowl add the cold water and gelatin together and let sit.

Next add 2 cups of heavy whipping cream and the vanilla bean to a medium size pot and scald.

While the cream is scalding whisk together the egg yolks and sugar in a large bowl until completely combined.

Once the cream has scalded slowly pour it into the egg yolk and sugar mixture to temper it while whisking.

Pour the mixture back in the pot and return it to the burner and constantly whisk over medium heat until it becomes thick.

Next, whisk in the gelatin/water mixture and chill completely.

Serve in martini glasses top with fresh berries and powdered sugar.

BRISKET

Description

It just would not be Hanukkah without a traditional Brisket. I find that an unseasoned canned tomato sauce, such as Hunt's works well for this recipe. The best secret of all: make this one or two days before serving, so you have more time to spend with your guests.

Ingredients

4-5 lbs. flat cut brisket
1 1/2 tsp. garlic salt
1 Tbsp. all-purpose flour
4 large Vidalia onions sliced
1/4 cup canola or vegetable oil
1-2 tsp. ground black pepper
2-3 Tbsp. Hungarian paprika
1 (.13 oz.) packet of beef seasoning or beef base (my mom always used G Washington broth packets)
1 (8 oz.) can of unseasoned tomato sauce
A hearty portion of time and love!

Directions

Heat the Canola oil in a non-stick Dutch oven at medium high temperature.
Add the sliced onions and sauté until golden brown and caramelized, stirring often (about 15 minutes).
Season the onions with 1/2 tsp. of garlic salt and 1/2 tsp. of black pepper. Remove from pot. Add 2 more Tbsp. of Canola oil IF NEEDED.
Season the brisket on both sides with garlic salt, black pepper, Hungarian paprika and the all-purpose flour.
Add the brisket to the heated Dutch oven and sear the meat on both sides, approximately 5-7 minutes per side.
Reduce the heat to a simmer.
Add the caramelized onions, one 8 oz. can of unseasoned tomato sauce and 1 individual packet of beef base and cover.
Simmer approximately 2 1/2 hours, turning the brisket over one time.
Remove the brisket from the pot and place on a heavy plate.
Place a heavy platter on top of the brisket and refrigerate overnight.
Separately refrigerate the pot with the au jus overnight also.
Before reheating, skim any fat that has risen to the top and discard.
Reheat the au jus on medium low heat.
Slice the brisket against the grain. Add to the hot au jus until warm, about 10 minutes.
Cooking tip:
The grain in briskets often changes while slicing, so continually reposition the brisket and slice against the grain.

CARROT CAKE PANCAKES

Description

Carrot cake was a big seller at our cafes. My love of pancakes keeps this a Sunday morning special.

Ingredients

1 1/4 cups all-purpose flour
1/4 cup chopped walnuts, toasted
2 tsp. baking powder
1 tsp. ground cinnamon
1/4 tsp. salt
1/8 tsp. freshly ground nutmeg
Dash of ground cloves
Dash of ground ginger
1/4 cup brown sugar
3/4 cup low-fat buttermilk
1 Tbsp. canola oil
1 1/2 tsp. vanilla extract
2 large eggs, lightly beaten
2 cups finely grated carrot (about 1 lb.)
Cooking spray
3 Tbsp. butter softened
2 Tbsp. honey

Directions

Combine flour, walnuts, baking powder, cinnamon, salt, nutmeg, cloves and ginger in a large bowl, stirring with a whisk.

Combine 1/4 cup brown sugar and next 4 ingredients (through eggs); add sugar mixture to flour mixture, stirring until just moist. Fold in 2 cups carrot.

Heat a large, nonstick skillet over medium heat.

Coat pan with cooking spray.

Spoon 4 (1/4 cup) batter mounds onto pan, spreading with a spatula.

Cook for 2 minutes or until tops are covered with bubbles and edges look cooked. Carefully turn pancakes over; cook 1 minute or until bottoms are lightly browned. Repeat procedure twice with remaining batter.

Combine butter and honey in a small bowl, serve with pancakes.

RIVA'S ZUCCHINI BREAD

Ingredients

2 tsp. butter for greasing the pans
3 to 4 cups grated fresh zucchini
3 cups (390 g) all-purpose flour
2 tsp. baking soda
2 tsp. cinnamon
1/2 tsp. ground ginger
1 1/3 cup (sugar
2 eggs, beaten
2 tsp. pure vanilla extract
1/2 tsp. salt
3/4 cup unsalted butter, melted
1 cup walnuts
Soft cream cheese

Directions

Preheat oven to 350 degrees °F.

Butter two 5 by 9-inch loaf pans.

Place the grated zucchini in a colander over a bowl to drain any excess moisture.

In a large bowl, whisk together the flour, baking soda, cinnamon and ginger,

In another large bowl, whisk together the sugar, eggs, vanilla extract, and salt. Stir in the drained grated zucchini and then the melted butter.

Add the flour mixture, a third at a time, to the sugar egg zucchini mixture, stirring after each incorporation. Fold in the nuts and dried cranberries or raisins if using.

Divide the batter equally between the loaf pans.

Bake for 50 minutes at 350 degrees °F or until a tester inserted into the center comes out clean.

Cool in pans for 10 minutes.

Turn out onto wire racks to cool thoroughly.

Serve with softened cream cheese.

MATZO BALL SOUP

Description

While I can't guarantee it will cure the common cold, it couldn't hurt. I think matzo ball soup is wonderful to serve year-round, whether you're celebrating Passover or just need some comfort in your life.

Ingredients

3 cartons chicken stock
1 whole chicken, rinsed and inside packet removed. k1 1/2 onions, cut into large chunks
4 stalks celery, leaves on, cut into large pieces
4 carrots, peeled, cut into large pieces
2 Tbsp. fresh dill, chopped
1 tsp. dill seed
1 Tbsp. poultry seasoning
1 tsp. celery seed

2 tsp. celery salt
Fresh ground pepper
Kosher salt, if needed
Fresh parsley
1 packet matzo ball mix
2 Tbsp. vegetable oil
2 eggs, beaten
4 qt. boiling water

Directions

Place the chicken stock, vegetables and seasoning in a soup pot.
Add chicken breasts and bring to a boil, then simmer for 20-25 minutes.
Remove chicken, cool slightly, remove skin and pull chicken meat off the bone into small pieces.
Return to pot.
In a separate bowl, mix 2 beaten eggs with 2 Tbsp. vegetable oil.
Add matzo ball mix and stir well.
Place in refrigerator for 20 minutes.
Boil 4 qt. water.
Take the matzo ball mix out of the refrigerator and roll into small balls. (I keep my hands wet so the matzo balls don't stick.)
Drop into boiling water, lower heat to a low boil, cover and cook for 20 minutes.
Remove the matzo balls from the boiling water and add to the soup.
Simmer soup for 30 minutes, adjust seasoning with salt and pepper and enjoy!

CREAM OF MUSHROOM SOUP

Description

To think I would not eat mushrooms as a child! While Nana preferred a mushroom barley soup, this was a staple at my restaurants and dinner table.

Ingredients

5 oz. fresh shiitake mushrooms
5 oz. fresh portobello mushrooms
5 oz. fresh cremini (or porcini) mushrooms
5 oz. fresh button mushrooms
48 oz. organic chicken stock
1 Tbsp. Extra virgin olive oil
1/4 lb. (1 stick) plus 1 Tbsp. truffle butter - divided
1 cup chopped yellow onion
1 sprig fresh thyme plus 1 tsp. minced
thyme leaves, divided

Kosher salt
Freshly ground black pepper
2 cups chopped leeks, white and
light green parts (2 leeks)
1/4 cup all-purpose flour
1 cup half-and-half
1 cup heavy cream
1/2 cup minced fresh flat-leaf parsley

Directions

Clean the mushrooms by wiping them with a dry paper towel. Don't wash them! Separate the stems, trim off any bad parts, and coarsely chop the stems. Slice the mushroom caps 1/4-inch thick and, if there are big, cut them into bite-sized pieces.
Set aside.
To make the stock:
Heat the olive oil and 1 Tbsp. of the truffle butter in a large pot.
Add the chopped mushroom stems, the onion, the sprig of thyme, 1 tsp. salt, and 1/2 tsp. pepper and cook over medium-low heat for 10 to 15 minutes, until the vegetables are soft.
Add 48 oz. of organic chicken stock, bring to a boil, reduce the heat, and simmer uncovered for 30 minutes.
Meanwhile, in another large pot, heat the remaining 1/4 lb. of butter and add the leeks.
Cook over low heat for 15 minutes, until the leeks begin to brown.
Add the sliced mushroom caps and cook for 10 minutes, or until they are browned and tender.
Add the flour and cook for 1 minute.
Add the mushroom stock, minced thyme leaves, 1 1/2 tsp. salt, and fresh ground pepper and bring to a boil.
Reduce the heat and simmer for 15 minutes.
Add the half-and-half, cream, and parsley, season with salt and pepper, to taste, and heat through but do not boil.
Garnish with fresh flat-leaf parsley.
Serve hot.
Note:
This soup tends to thicken up overnight in the refrigerator, as you reheat slowly add hot chicken stock until it is slightly thick and creamy.

SOUR-CREAM BLUEBERRY COFFEE CAKE

Description

Every family has that recipe that is handed down. I adore sour cream coffee cake warm out of the oven. You can add blackberries and cranberries as well.

Ingredients

2 sticks sweet butter
2 cups granulated sugar
2 eggs, beaten
2 cups unbleached all-purpose flour
1 Tbsp. baking powder
1/4 tsp. salt

2 cups dairy sour cream
1 tsp. pure vanilla extract
3/4 cup brown sugar
1 1/2 Tbsp. ground cinnamon
1 1/2 cups shelled pecans, chopped
1 cup fresh blueberries

Directions

Preheat oven to 350 degrees °F.
Grease a 10 inch bundt pan or two 8 inch loaf pans.
Dust lightly with flour.
Cream together the butter and granulated sugar.
Add the beaten eggs and blend.
Add the sour cream, one cup at a time and add vanilla.
Sift together flour, baking powder and salt.
Fold the dry ingredients into the creamed mixture and beat until blended. Do not over mix.
In a separate bowl, mix brown sugar, chopped pecans and cinnamon together.
Pour half of the batter into the greased and floured pan.
Sprinkle half the brown sugar mixture on top.
Add 1/2 of the blueberries and pour the remaining batter into the pan.
Repeat the process with the remaining brown sugar mixture and fruit.
Place in the preheated oven in middle rack for approximately 45 to 50 minutes or until a cake tester comes out clean.
Let rest for about 45 minutes and serve while still warm.

SWEET AND SOUR STUFFED CABBAGE

Description

There is nothing that makes me happier then when my brother Glenn Cooper comes to visit. I usually run to the store and stock up on smoked white fish salad and lox, bagels and blintzes. Then of course there is the family stuffed cabbage recipe. Sweet with raisins and always served with red parsley potatoes, just like Mom and Nana made and one of Glenn's favorite dishes.

Ingredients

One large, green cabbage
2 lb. ground beef
1 cup cooked white rice
1 small onion chopped fine
Garlic salt to taste
2 15-oz. cans of Hunt's tomato sauce

1 egg
2 Tbsp. brown sugar
Kosher salt as needed
Fresh ground Black pepper to taste
1 cup raisins

Directions

Preheat oven to 350 degrees °F.

Combine the ground beef, rice, onion, garlic and egg. Mix well.

Place the cabbage in a boiling pot of water and steam until leaves begin to "peel" from the core. Remove cabbage leaves as they become tender, each time placing the head back in the pot to cook more inner leaves.Remove the tough middle core if needed on each piece. Pile the leaves in a large colander to remove excess water then set aside.

Place a cabbage leaf on a cutting board or counter and place a few Tbsp. of the meat mixture on the leaf near the bottom; Fold the bottom of the leaf up around the filling, then fold in the sides and roll up the leaf into a neat package. Set the filled rolls aside, seam side down. You can make meatballs with any leftover meat.

Combine the tomato sauce with lemon juice, brown sugar, salt and pepper in a bowl and mix well. Add raisins and adjust sweetness to your liking.

Place 3/4 of the sauce in a large baking dish and top with remaining sauce.

Cover and Bake in 350 degrees °F oven for 2 hours.

Serve with boiled and buttered red parsley potatoes.

My Mom usually used a stove top method with a large Dutch oven. I find the oven method is less messy and the cabbage rolls, or "bundles" as we called them brown nicely.

Nana loved using sour salt, a citric acid with the consistency of table salt.

PRIME RIB

Description

We ate a lot of roast beef in my childhood home. Prime Rib is not just for holidays. We often mid-week roast to have leftovers for sandwiches. I asked the butchers what holiday cooking questions they get asked the most and this is what they said: PRIME RIB!!! The absolute key is to have a calibrated oven and a good working meat thermometer.

Take the roast out of the refrigerator and leave at room temperature for 2 hours before roasting-this is VERY important.

Perfect prime rib is an easy undertaking if you follow a few key steps. The most important is using an accurate digital thermometer. This is the only way to ensure the desired doneness, which hopefully is a perfectly pink medium-rare, when the flavor and texture are at their best.

This prime rib recipe will work no matter what size roast you're using. A great rule of thumb is each rib will feed 2 guests. So, a 4 rib roast will serve 8 guests.

Ingredients

1 standing beef rib roast (4 to 7 ribs, approximately 9 lbs.)
Fresh coarse-ground black pepper, as needed
Kosher salt (or other larger grain, flake-style salt), 1/2 tsp. per bone—I prefer truffle salt with the black pepper and be generous

Softened butter, 1/2 tbsp per rib of beef
Large metal roasting pan with at least 3-inch sides.
2 Tbsp. flour
1 qt. cold beef broth

Directions

Preheat oven to 500 degrees °F.

Let sit at room temp for 1 ½ to two hours.

Make a rub of salt, pepper and truffle salt and apply to meat liberally all over.

Place meat in a shallow roasting pan fat side up.

Rub soft butter on both ends to seal in the juices.

Roast at 550°F at 5 minutes per pound for RARE, or 6 minutes per pound for MEDIUM. Turn off oven at the end of cooking time and DO NOT OPEN OVEN DOOR FOR TWO HOURS.

At the end of the 2 hours, remove meat from oven let rest for a half an hour before slice; it comes out perfect every time.

Works the same with Roast beef. The next time you want an easy hands-off, tender and juicy roast, try this recipe - you won't be disappointed!

To Make the "Au Jus" Sauce

While the prime rib is resting, pour off all but 2 tablespoons of the fat from the pan and place on the stovetop over medium heat.

Add the flour and cook, stirring, for 5 minutes to form a roux.

Pour in the beef broth and whisk into the roux, scraping all the caramelized beef drippings from the bottom of the pan.

Turn heat to high and cook the sauce for 10 minutes until it reduces and thickens slightly (this is not a gravy, so don't expect a thick, heavy sauce).

Adjust seasoning, strain and serve alongside the prime rib.

Chapter Three

THE EARLY YEARS

There was always something seductive about the aroma of food routinely simmering and baking in my childhood home. Why, by the age of five, I was sneaking extra oregano and garlic into my Mother's sauce. For some innate reason, at this early age, there was something gravitating about adding pinches of this and that. Every Wednesday (just like the Prince Spaghetti commercial), Mom would unveil that yummy homemade tomato sauce, which had been lovingly prepared in the height of tomato season. Gathered from the freezer, the soothing sauce, completed with ground beef and sweet Italian sausages, turned predictability into purpose.

There was always homemade garlic bread and a salad....a fine salad. Every single night, a composed salad, a wedge of lettuce with Russian dressing or, my favorite, a mixed salad - iceberg, cucumbers, tomatoes red onions and homemade Russian dressing. Nightly in my home, despite a maniacal Father who could erupt at an unforeseen second, there was a salad: my nurturing Mother's attempt at securing order and comfort. Alas, the power and promise of food.

My teacher for second and third grade was Mrs. Fletcher. A big coup that she moved up a grade at the same time I did. She was a lovely older woman with rosy cheeks and full of hugs and good spirit. Her favorite poem about a juicy red apple was displayed on poster board and when I closed my eyes I could taste the crispness, the tartness that I so loved about autumn apples. So what if it was a picture of a Delicious apple not McIntosh. For me, a description alone made me crave apple pie, apple turnovers and Nana's apple strudel. Just hearing a narration of food was my little comfort place and I could begin to smell certain aromas by simply thinking about a piece of fruit....and what it might become with butter, cinnamon, sugar and pie crust.

Of course, these venerated recollections are offset with nightmares of an unstable Father, who, from time to time, would choose dinnertime to throw plates against a wall and order us to our rooms for not appreciating what he never had. In his head, we became ungrateful children, spoiled with little care that he had to eat potatoes for days when he was our age.

Perhaps it was living with the trepidation that made me such a persnickety eater. In my family, as most Jewish families in the 60's, going out for fresh high-end Chinese food was invariably a Sunday night tradition. At the time, captious Judi refused to try anything but a sparerib. Yes, I was more than a picky child when it came to food. Roast beef- yes, corn- yes (the only veg other than salad), and, when all else failed, a Bumble Bee tuna sandwich made with Hellman's Mayonnaise and chopped celery on toasted rye with lettuce and tomato. This fastidious relationship with food soon evolved into a sense of ownership, safety and identity.

October 8, 1968: my first Easy Bake Oven. The best birthday present that this fussy child with an adult palate could possibly get. There were little bags of mixes, little pans, little tiny spatulas and the big light bulb that became the heat for MY creation of pastries. By week two, I was mastering the art of the chocolate layer cake, albeit the size of a mouse, stacked with layers of Smucker's strawberry jelly.

Knowing that my product was as good as the Baked Goods Department at Highland Park Market, the bold entrepreneur set a table outside with Zyrex mixed with pink lemonade as the drink of the day and sold two bite size cakes to the postman for a whopping 25 cents. Off and running, my first legitimate bakery. Soon, I could bang out 4 cakes a day as long as Mom could take me to Caldor's to stock up on the mixes.

I was obsessed. Sensing that the lightbulb-baking might not keep up with the supply and demand of the mailman and garbage man, I decided to read a cookbook my Mom had on a shelf in the kitchen. Oatmeal raisin cookies looked good. I grabbed the stool, went into every cabinet and made a note of which ingredients might be lacking. When I saw the vanilla extract, I closed my eyes and could smell the wonderful brown liquid, like when Mom added it to her French toast batter; the same sensation I had during Mrs. Fletcher's reading of the big juicy apple. Ingredients just seemed to flow through my mind, my soul was animated by spices and scents.

Fearing the loss of a limb, my over-worrisome Mom limited me to the hand mixer instead of the glass bowl machine. Nevertheless, whatever it took, I made it happen: the butter and sugar creamed, the egg fluffed up the batter, the oats, raisins and brown sugar became magically entrenched. I baked for everyone on the street that I possibly could -- plates of homemade oatmeal cookies, and then chocolate fudge brownies, followed by toll house cookies. While business was brisk, no one at home seemed to notice the difference between my great cookies and that of the Fig Newton. How could my family open box after box of those things and not taste cardboard and muck? Why turn away a warm delicious cookie with just the right crispness around the edges for something that could be dunked in a glass of milk and never lose its shape?

Stranger in my homeland, alone in my own culinary world of all things butter and homemade, I immersed myself in baking.

That is, until my first dinner party.

CHICKEN & CORN FLAKES

Descriptions

This was a winner for my first dinner party. The key is to soak the chicken overnight in buttermilk to make it extra juicy. While Nana and Mom used a can of condensed milk, I prefer buttermilk. Do make sure you use Kellogg's cornflakes as they are slightly sweeter than other brands. My Mom's own version of Shake n Bake.The best part of this simple recipe is picking at the corn flakes stuck to the pan. As siblings, we would fight for the extra crispy pieces left in the pan.

Ingredients

1 box Kellogg's cornflakes
crushed fine
2 quarts buttermilk
4 bone in chicken breasts
4 bone in chicken thighs
4 chicken legs
Kosher salt
Garlic slat
Fresh ground black pepper
Paprika

Directions

Drain chicken from buttermilk.
Add one piece at a time to crushed seasoned corn flakes.
Shake well in brown paper bag. Lay on a broiler pan fitted with aluminum foil. Spray foil with PAM
Season with extra garlic salt and paprika.
Bake at 375 degrees °F for 45-50 minutes until crisp.

CAULIFLOWER PUREE

Description

While I grew up eating potatoes or noodle pudding most nights, I much prefer cauliflower and carrot purees to mashed potatoes any day.

Ingredients

8 large cloves garlic minced
2 Tbsp. butter
5-6 cups cauliflower florets
5-6 cups vegetable broth or water

1 tsp. Kosher salt (more to taste)
1/2 tsp. fresh ground pepper (more to taste)
1/2 cup milk
Pinch of gravy master

Directions

Sauté the minced garlic with the butter in a large nonstick skillet over low heat.

Cook for several minutes or until the garlic is soft and fragrant but not browned (browned or burnt garlic will taste bitter).

Remove from heat and set aside.

Cauliflower:

Bring the water or vegetable broth to a boil in a large pot.

Add the cauliflower and cook, covered, for 7-10 minutes or until cauliflower is fork tender. Do not drain.

Puree:

Use a slotted spoon to transfer the cauliflower pieces to the blender.

Add 1 cup vegetable broth or cooking liquid, sautéed garlic/butter, salt, pepper, and milk.

Blend or puree for several minutes until the sauce is very smooth, adding more broth or milk depending on how thick you want the sauce.

You may have to do this in batches depending on the size of your blender.

Add a drop of gravy master and Serve hot!

If the sauce starts to look dry, add a few drops of water, milk, or olive oil.

CHOPPED SALAD

Ingredients

1 head iceberg lettuce, chopped
3 tomatoes, quartered
2 English cucumbers, peeled and diced
1/2 red onion, diced
1 cup Lars onion slivers
4 hard cooked eggs, chopped

Directions

Toss with Avocado dressing or
Riva's favorite:
Hellmans Mayo
Heinz ketchup
Garlic salt
Mix together and toss into chopped salad

AVOCADO CILANTRO DRESSING

Ingredients

1/2 avocado, ripe
3/4 cup cilantro, packed
1/2 cup nonfat plain yogurt
2 scallions, chopped

1 garlic clove, quartered
1 Tbsp. lime juice
1/2 tsp. sugar
1/2 tsp. salt

Directions

Puree all in blender until smooth.
Adjust seasoning with salt and pepper as needed.

DATE NUT BREAD

Description

When I was a child my Mom would serve me Date Nut Bread with Philadelphia Cream Cheese before I went to morning or afternoon Kindergarten. I loved the taste. Sticky and slightly sweet but the cream cheese was just the perfect touch, especially for a child that would not eat a PBJ.

Ingredients

1 cup pitted chopped dates
6 dried figs chopped
1 cup coarsely chopped walnuts
1 1/2 tsp. baking soda
1/2 tsp. salt
3 Tbsp. vegetable shortening

3/4 cup boiling water
2 eggs
3/4 cup sugar
1/2 cup whole wheat flour
1 cup all-purpose flour

Directions

Preheat the oven to 350 degrees °F.

Grease an 8 1/2 x 4 1/2 x 3 inch loaf pan.

Put the dates, walnuts, baking soda, salt and shortening in a bowl. Pour the boiling water over and stir. Let the mixture stand for 15 minutes.

Using a fork beat the eggs and sugar together in a bowl.

Add the flours and stir; the batter will be too stiff to mix well.

Add the chopped dates and figs and mix briskly until the batter is well blended.

Spoon into the loaf pan and bake 40 to 50 minutes.

The date nut bread is done when a few moist crumbs cling to a straw inserted in the middle of the loaf.

The bread will continue to bake after it is removed from the oven. Do not overbake, or the loaf will be dry.

When the loaf is done, slide a knife around the edges of the pan and turn the loaf onto a rack to cool completely.

Serve with smooth and creamy cream cheese.

EGGPLANT ROLLATINE

Description

I thought eggplant was actually a meat. Mom never told me otherwise since I liked it so much but was a finicky vegetable eater. A change from parmesan, I love any dish that includes ricotta cheese and eggplant.

Ingredients

4 eggplants, sliced on mandolin
Sprinkle with kosher salt and drain in
colander to remove moisture
1 bunch fresh basil
1 jar Michaels from Brooklyn sauce
or fresh homemade sauce
1 (8 oz.) container fresh ricotta (not reduced fat)
Salt and pepper to taste
3 Tbsp. sun dried tomatoes, drained from oil

Garlic salt
Fresh sliced mozzarella
1 cup shaved Parmesan, saving a few lunches for garnish
1 egg beaten
Olive oil
1 (8 oz.) pack fresh organic arugula.
Zest of one lemon.
Juice of two lemons.

Directions

Preheat oven to 350 degrees °F.
Mix Parmesan with ricotta and garlic salt. Add fresh picked basil and beaten egg.
Pat eggplant dry and place on a cookie sheet and bake until tender and slightly brown, about 6 to 8 minutes.
Remove from oven and place eggplant on cutting board or counter.
Take a Tbsp. or 2 of ricotta mixture and place on top of a piece of sliced eggplant. Roll and repeat until all mixture is used.
Spray a baking sheet with food spray and pour bottom with fresh sauce. Add layer of eggplant stuffed with cheese mixture.
Top with a spoon of sauce on each rollatini and sliced fresh mozzarella.
Bake at 350 degrees °F until cheese melts.
In a separate bowl mix arugula with lemon juice, lemon zest and a sprinkle of EVOO.
Toss well.
Place 2 rollatinis on plate and top with arugula salad.
Garnish with fresh basil and shredded Parmesan.

HEARTY BEEF STEW

Description

True, I refused to eat any braised meats as a child. This was Hilary's comfort in a bowl favorite. Needless to say, I traded her my bowl for her extra bread and butter. Somewhere between a beef stew and a classic beef Bourguignon, this recipe was born.

Number One Rule - Use a good quality stew meat like Hereford Beef

Number Two Rule - Use a good Cabernet

Ingredients

2 lbs. stew meat, cut into cubes
Approximately 1/4 cup all-purpose flour
Garlic salt and fresh ground black pepper
1/4 cup canola or vegetable oil
1.5 oz. container of Demi-Glace Gold (this brand is only $4.99 and well worth it for a rich hearty stock)
2-3 cups hot water
1 cup plus rich cabernet wine
1 cup baby carrots
1 cup sliced celery

2 cups peeled fresh baby onions
1 cup cut red potatoes
1/2 cup dried porcini mushrooms
1 bay leaf
1 cup frozen peas - thawed but not cooked
Buttered noodles - cooked

To thicken if needed:
1 tsp. cornstarch
1/2 cup cold water

Directions

Heat oil in large pot.
Season meat with garlic salt and black pepper.
Let rest 5 minutes or so.
Toss gently into flour shaking off excess before adding to pot.
Gently brown on both sides.
Add water and demi-glace mix.
Lower heat and simmer for 30 minutes.
Add wine and simmer another 30 minutes.
Add red potatoes, onions, carrots and celery.
Adjust seasoning and add more wine if needed.
Simmer until vegetables are tender.
Add peas and taste to see if you would like the stew thicker or more seasoned.
Remove bay leaf.
Add slurry to low boiling stew if you need to thicken.
Serve over buttered noodles.

MARINARA SAUCE

Description

In the summer my Mom use to buy baskets of fresh Roma tomatoes that signified "sauce day". I would run into the kitchen grab my stool and start stirring the pot knowing that night we would have the perfect pasta dish ready for dinner!

Ingredients

1/4 cup extra virgin olive oil
1 (28 oz.) can whole tomatoes, chopped
Kosher salt and fresh ground black pepper
1 medium onion, diced

1/2 cup garlic cloves, peeled and
minced (use only fresh garlic)
12 large fresh basil leaves torn

Directions

Add EVOO in a large stainless-steel saucepan.
Add onion and garlic over medium heat and sauté, stirring frequently until tender and translucent (**do not brown**).
Add the chopped tomatoes (I buy high quality canned whole tomatoes and use a French knife into the can to chop.)
Simmer approx. 20 to 30 minutes, stirring often.
Season with Kosher salt and fresh ground black pepper.
Add basil leaves and remove from heat.
Stir well then cover tightly.
Optional:
1/2 tsp. dried oregano
Pinch of crushed red pepper flakes

MODERN BOLOGNESE SAUCE

Ingredients

4 links sweet Italian sausage, casings removed
2 links hot Italian sausage, casings removed
2 1/2 lbs.- 3 lbs. ground chuck
1 onion chopped
1 green pepper, diced
1 red pepper diced
1 cup half and half
1/3 cup dry Italian red wine
Garlic salt to taste
4 cloves garlic peeled and chopped
Large batch Marinara-
(or for a cheat I use Michael's of Brooklyn sauce- 3 jars)
EVOO

Directions

In a large heavy pot, heat 2 Tbsp. Extra Virgin Olive oil.

Add ground sausage and begin to brown, using large metal spoon to break up. Add ground beef (not too lean).

Season with garlic salt. Drain excess fat.

Add onions, garlic and peppers. Stir but do not let brown.

Add Marinara sauce (or cheat sauce but ONLY Michael's of Brooklyn)

Simmer stirring about every 20 minutes for 3-4 hours.

Season with salt, pepper and a pinch of crushed red pepper if needed.

In the last 1/2 hour add 1 cup of half and half and simmer on low heat for another 20 minutes.

Personally, I sauté zucchini noodles for about 2 minutes in EVOO then pour the meat sauce over the top and garnish with a Tablespoon of ricotta cheese.

Note:
You can add a box of Pomi tomato puree if there is not enough liquid but I like it very meaty.

ORANGE POUND CAKE

Ingredients

1/2 lb. (2 sticks) unsalted butter, at room temperature
2 1/2 cups granulated sugar, divided
4 extra-large eggs, at room temperature
1/3 cup grated orange zest (6 oranges)
3 cups all-purpose flour
1/2 tsp. baking powder

1/2 tsp. baking soda
1 tsp. kosher salt
3/4 cup freshly squeezed orange juice, divided
3/4 cup buttermilk, at room temperature
1 tsp. pure vanilla extract

To glaze one loaf (optional):
1 cup confectioners' sugar, sifted

1 1/2 Tbsp. freshly squeezed orange juice

Directions

Heat the oven to 350 degrees °F.

Grease and flour two 8 1/2 x 4 1/2 x 2 1/2 inch loaf pans.

Line the bottoms with parchment paper.

Cream the butter and 2 cups of the granulated sugar in the bowl of an electric mixer fitted with the paddle attachment for about 5 minutes, or until light and fluffy.

With the mixer on medium speed, beat in the eggs, one at a time, and the orange zest.

In a large bowl, sift together the flour, baking powder, baking soda, and salt.

In another bowl, combine 1/4 cup of the orange juice, the buttermilk, and vanilla.

Add the flour and buttermilk mixtures alternately to the batter, beginning and ending with the flour.

Divide the batter evenly between the pans, smooth the tops, and bake for 45 minutes to 1 hour, until a cake tester comes out clean.

While the cakes bake, cook the remaining 1/2 cup of granulated sugar with the remaining 1/2 cup orange juice in a small saucepan over low heat until the sugar dissolves.

Cool cakes for 10 minutes before flipping pan onto a cooling rack.

Spoon the orange syrup over the cakes and allow the cakes to cool completely.

To glaze, combine the confectioners' sugar and orange juice in a bowl, mixing with a wire whisk until smooth.

Add a few more drops of juice, if necessary, to make it pour easily.

Pour over the top of one cake and allow the glaze to dry.

Wrap well, and store in the refrigerator.

PANKO CRUSTED FILLET OF SOLE WITH SUMO ORANGE BUTTER SAUCE

Description

My mother always bought fillet of sole only on Fridays from the fish market knowing it was the freshest. While she loved to dip it in egg, bread crumbs and pan fry, I added a more modern twist.

Ingredients

1 1/2 lb. fresh filet of sole
2 Sumo oranges (if they are out of season
use whatever is the sweetest)
4 sprigs fresh dill
1 tsp. drained capers
3 Tbsp. Irish butter
2 Tbsp. vegetable oil plus a few more if needed.
3 Tbsp. sumo orange ZEST
2 eggs beaten well
Dusting of flour

Fresh ground black pepper
Microgreens for garnish
2 Japanese potatoes peeled, cut into wedges and
boiled for 6 minutes to remove excess starch.
2 sweet potatoes cut into wedges.
Olive oil to taste.
No salt seasoning like Frontier or
Florida sunshine seasoning
2 cups baby kale-washed

Directions

Preheat oven to 400 degrees °F.
Toss potatoes in seasoning and olive oil and line a pan with parchment.
Spread on sheet and roast until crisp.
In a large pan add 2 Tbsp. veg oil and 2 Tbsp. butter.
Dip sole in egg wash then flour - shake off excess then dip in seasoned panko crumbs.
Pan sear until brown on both sides.
Plate over potato wedges and arrange fresh dill on top.
Remove from pan - wipe clean.
Add 2 tsp. veg oil and sliced Sumo oranges and 2 Tbsp. Irish butter.
Add capers and sauté.
Squeeze juice of one Sumo orange into pan.
Add kale and gently wilt.
Pour over fish and garnish with micro greens and orange zest.
Serve immediately.

PEACH, BLUEBERRY, RASPBERRY COBBLER

Ingredients

12 ripe peaches
1 pint blueberries
1 pt. raspberries
juice of half a lemon
1 Tbsp. flour
1 cup flour
1 cup sugar

2 eggs
1 tsp. cinnamon
1 stick melted butter
4 Tbsp. sugar
2 Tbsp. butter
Cinnamon and sugar for topping

Directions

Peel the peaches by blanching them in boiling water for 15 seconds or so and then running them under cold water. The skins will slip right off.

Slice them into a bowl, being sure to capture all the juice.

Add the blueberries and raspberries.

Stir flour into the sugar and stir the mixture into the fruit.

Add the lemon juice and give it another stir.

In a separate bowl mix equal parts of flour or sugar

Toss in 1/2 tsp. salt and 1 Tbsp. baking powder

Crack one egg at a time and form into a crumble.

Place over mixed fruit and top with melted butter. Bake until top is golden brown and top with ice cream.

Preheat oven to 375 degrees °F.

Spoon the blueberries, peaches and raspberries in individual crocks.

Top with crumble and drizzle melted butter.

Top with more cinnamon and sugar mixture

Bake until topping can be tapped on crumble top to make sure it is done.

Top with mango, coconut or blueberry ice cream ice cream.

RUGELACH

Description

A true labor of love-Warning, your family will attack as soon as they come out of the oven.

Ingredients

Dough:
16 Tbsp. (1 cup) unsalted butter, at room temperature
3/4 cup cream cheese, at room temperature
1/3 cup sour cream
1/2 tsp. salt
2 cups Unbleached All-Purpose Flour

Filling:
1/2 cup brown sugar
1 cup walnuts, chopped
1/2 cup dried cranberries, raisins, or currants
1 Tbsp. cinnamon
Water for brushing dough

Topping:
Granulated sugar or coarse white sparkling sugar
Milk or cream

Directions

To make the dough using a food processor:
Place the flour and salt in the bowl of a food processor.
Pulse briefly to combine.
Cut the butter and cream cheese into chunks and add to the bowl along with the sour cream.
Pulse just until the dough forms chunks, and you can squeeze it together.
To make the dough using a mixer:
Beat together the butter, cream cheese, sour cream, and salt until smooth.
Add the flour, mixing to make a stiff dough.
Divide the dough into three equal portions. Press each gently into a disk.
Make the disks as round as possible, smoothing their edges; this will allow you to roll the disks into a perfectly round circle.

Wrap the disks in plastic, and chill the dough for about 1 hour, until it's firm. Or chill longer (up to overnight), then warm for about 45 to 60 minutes at room temperature, until the dough softens enough to roll out without cracking.

To make the filling, process the sugar, walnuts, dried fruit, and cinnamon in a food processor or blender until finely chopped and well combined.

Working with one piece of dough at a time, place it on a generously floured surface.

Roll it into a 10" circle and brush it lightly with water.

Use your fingers to spread about 1/3 of the filling onto the round, going all the way to the edges and gently patting the filling to help anchor it to the dough.

Using a sharp knife, divide the dough into 12 equal wedges.

Roll each wedge up, beginning with the wide end and ending with the narrow end.

Place the rolls point-side down on a baking sheet; lining the baking sheet with parchment will help with cleanup. Repeat with the remaining two pieces of dough.

Brush the rugelach with milk or cream; and sprinkle with granulated or coarse white sparkling sugar, if desired.

Preheat the oven to 350 degrees °F.

Refrigerate the rugelach while the oven is preheating.

Bake the rugulach for 25 to 30 minutes, or until golden brown.

Remove from the oven, and cool right on the pan.

Serve warm or at room temperature.

Warning your hard work will be devoured in 10 minutes!

SAUTÉED VEGGIE POCKETS

Description

I made these at the Main Street Café so that we would have a vegetarian choice. I found people just loved the way the swiss melted into the grilled veggies enough that they didn't miss the meat. Have fun with this and shop your produce drawer.

Ingredients

2 Whole pita breads cut in half
1 tsp. olive oil
2 Tbsp. olive oil
1 clove garlic minced
8 slices Swiss cheese
4 slices Provolone
1 Vidalia or other sweet onion
1/3 red onion julienned
2 red peppers, julienned
2 green peppers julienned
1 8-oz. package of fresh mushrooms sliced
8 slices ripe red tomatoes
Fresh spinach
Broccoli sprouts

Directions

Heat large pan with olive oil. Add garlic but do not brown.
Add sliced onions, peppers and mushrooms and sauté until veggies are slightly tender but still a little crisp.
Heat griddle pan.
Place desired amount of swiss cheese and provolone in pockets and brush outside with olive oil.
Stuff with grilled veggies and flip once to warm the pita bread and melt the cheese into the veggies.
Stuff with sliced tomatoes and fresh spinach and broccoli sprouts.

STUFFED FRENCH TOAST WITH WARM PEACH BLUEBERRY COMPOTE

Description

While most people think of French Toast as a brunch or breakfast item, I often serve this warming dish as a dessert. Frozen peaches and frozen mixed berries are just as good as fresh.

Ingredients

1 loaf Challah bread, sliced thick
1 lb. cream cheese, softened
1/2 cup Mascarpone cheese (Italian cream cheese)
3 Tbsp. plus powdered sugar
1 tsp. pure vanilla extract
2 Tbsp. Grand Marnier liquor
3 eggs beaten
1/2 cup whole milk

1 Tbsp. ground cinnamon
1 tsp. pure vanilla extract
2 cups fresh or frozen peaches and mixed berries
Unsalted butter (approximately 6 Tbsp. split)
1/4 cup brown sugar

Directions

Whip softened cream cheese, mascarpone and vanilla extract with powdered sugar – Spread mixture between two slices of Challah Bread.

Whip eggs with milk, cinnamon and 1 tsp. vanilla extract in a large bowl.

Preheat electric fry pan or large pan to medium high.

Add 1-2 Tbsp. butter. (Do not brown the butter)

Dip stuffed bread into batter mixture and lightly brown on both sides.

Remove from pan and repeat.

Cut the stuffed French Toast into quarters and arrange on a platter.

Add remaining butter and melt.

Add brown sugar and blend with butter.

Deglaze pan with Grand Marnier and add frozen fruit.

Continue to stir until a thick compote has blended and the fruit is warm.

Pour over French Toast and serve immediately.

Chapter Four

THE EDUCATION OF A CHEF

Many children know what they want to be when they grow up. For me, I never quite knew that females could be professional chefs until I saw Julia Child on TV. My mother and I watched her faithfully, along with the Galloping Gourmet, but the six foot woman in the starched PBS uniform was me. I could relate to someone who was that tall, found herself in a male's profession and never once imagined or wanted to be on TV. (Who knew…?)

Chefs didn't come out of the kitchen where my family ate. They were far from rock stars. I never really thought about who was cooking my order when we went out. Of course, we only ate out for Chinese, Veal Parmesan and the bi-weekly dose of <u>Shady Glenn</u> Cheeseburgers and Coleslaw.

Ah…<u>Shady Glenn</u>: the grill man intrigued me there. He harbored in the restaurant for over 40 years, eventually buying out Bernice the original owner. I always wanted the booth closest to the grill, where I could watch him place sliced cheese on the grill as I simultaneously eyed the crusty cheesy goodness that was upcurled on top of the simple hamburger patty.

I just knew that I needed to cook and somehow, if my goal of being a rock n roll DJ didn't work out, if Bruce Springsteen and the E street band weren't quite big enough to afford a traveling rocking cook who made a good brisket, then somehow I needed something that allowed me to feed people. Clearly as often intimated from my mother, young girls in the 1960's and 70's had no place in a restaurant kitchen. My mother's goal was to see her youngest become a dietician, so I could work with food. Of course, my math and science skills were lacking and the thought of looking at soft foods on plastic trays did nothing more that petrify me.

Cooking became a hobby. Home Ec. was a total waste of my time. Broiling grapefruit with brown sugar was so last year. Reading cookbooks, watching the first PBS cooking shows and hosting dinner parties became my obsession. My neighbor and dear friend Paige Calhoun became my first guest, along with a few other neighborhood kids. If I recall correctly, we had canned fruit cocktail with a melon ball scoop of orange sherbert, (my Mother's forte) a salad with Russian dressing, baked stuffed potatoes and chicken and cornflakes, no doubt maybe even Pillsbury crescent rolls. Soon there were New Years Eve Cocktail parties with pigs in a blanket, canapes and, a fourth-grade special, English muffin pizzas.

I sealed my fate when in high school I went to College Night and met reps from The Culinary Institute of America and from Johnson and Wales. Sensing that Providence R.I. would have less snow and be closer to my friends at U Conn, I brought the J & W package home and begged my mother to support my culinary education path. I certainly was not the type of teenager to throw some clothes in a suitcase and head to Paris or Italy and intern nor were my parents the type to support such "suspicious" behavior. Rhode Island was close enough to New York and Boston, two great eating cities. It took a little while to convince my Mother, but after swooning her over with my eggplant parmesan and triple layer brown derby cake, my college fate was sealed.

Going to an esteemed culinary school is somewhat military. You wear starched uniforms with only white or black socks and professional steel toe shoes and have your knife bag contents inspected daily for sharpness and cleanliness. However, once the day was done, we were pretty much wild young college students doing our version of crazy dorm parties, like sneaking in a banned box of hot pots to make bolognese sauce with gnocchi or beef bourguignon with buttered noodles. Dorm cafeteria food in a culinary school is surprisingly awful and, like my friends up the street at Brown University, dinner parties with obscure cooking instruments were iconic.

To make "cooking money" for the week, I worked at a diner most Sat nights (when I wasn't in Jersey following the E Street Band). The end of night free cheeseburger club and coffee milk made the sexual harassment kind of worth it to a young, naive college kid. Working as a server, the grill cooks were mean and crude, although I could easily have taught them how to make crispier fries. Perhaps they resented my comments when I would refuse to serve a burger that was supposed to be medium rare, but seemed to become a shrunken dry piece of cardboard. At 2:00 am in Providence, R.I., most "guests" didn't really care, other than this 'know it all' server. Coffee milk and stuffed quahogs, the official food of Providence, became my preferred dining options when not creating something simmering with our illegal cooking instruments.

With some gumption I managed to score an internship at the restaurant the college owned and ended up cooking along with many of my instructors (aka fellow Heineken drinkers). They taught me so much. Rule number one: you burn yourself when the butter foams over the pan ('too bad', there is no time for ice or cold water). It is your war wound and many a wound I did wear! However, I learned how to sauté many different pans filled with various deliciousness and finishing sauces at various stages of completion that it was one of the best learning experiences of my working career. No doubt I could have stayed at Johnson and Wales for many more years, but they did not offer Masters in "hot pot dorm cooking", nor any Masters at the Culinary School. It was time to polish up the metal toe shoes and get a real job.

Most Culinary students did not expect to come out as a "Chef", though there were a good number of rich kids who were all set, as the parents owned 9 restaurants. Most like me, however, learned you had to earn it. Five years in, lugging 50 pound bags of onions, sugar and lots and lots of garbage, you were fortunate if someone remembered your name, let alone show you a little respect.

Let me remind you, graduating in 1980 and entering a world of hot kitchens with only men in charge was not exactly a 5 star Michelin experience. Although many jobs are offered at graduation, the women were offered pantry station, slicing and plating desserts, and assembling salads. The men all had the high chef hats, sizzling pans and screaming lungs. Sexism ran like bulls chasing red flags down the streets, and getting to the sauté station took more than skills. You had to balance 9 orders cooking at various stages with some self-entitled male yelling your last name. Any man on the line was treated much differently – slaps on the back, high fives, etc.. They would hand their dirtiest pans for us to clean, often while unconsciously grabbing their crotch.

I mastered the sauté station: sizzling, searing, reducing and deglazing created a beat like music to me and I somehow kept up with the flow. The fact that most men would not joke, be social in any way or do more than their share made me more competitive. Plus being over 6 feet had to create some feeling of "don't mess with the tall one".

After graduation, I took a few easy summer jobs, like bartending, before moving to Massachusetts and settling into my first marriage. Lesson to the young-do not buy furniture or get married before 30, your tastes will change. I spent a few years in the corporate world, honing the paperwork and knowledge of profits and losses, before we borrowed the money to buy a small café in Gloucester, MA.

The café was almost an instant success. Main Street Café featured a little salad bar, all homemade dressings, four types of homemade soup every day, hand cut Romanian pastrami and those classic Jordan Marsh homemade muffins. We had lines out the door, a sassy waitress who promised the attorneys that she would never tell their wives about their cinnamon roll consumption, as their other sins of lunch 5 days a week. She also made a damn good pie. I mean the type of apple or peach pie where you envision a farmer's wife in Iowa, placing the pies to cool on a red and white checkered cloth on the window sill. Martha Graham was a pistol and fabulous cook. Together, we undertook the next business step of catering. With my height of 6'1" and Martha's of 5 feet solid, we called ourselves "The Long and the Short of it Catering". Our motto was: "No job too big or too small." It was a nice project that fostered creative instincts. Business was so good that I asked my husband at the time to join the restaurant…..not a good move. Working closely with someone who, shall we say, might not exude a constructive approach is not a good business decision. While I smoothed things over with a frustrated server or begged forgiveness for overcooking someone's poached eggs, I found myself alone. Eventually, It was time to sell. The banks knew what we had accomplished, for future ventures, much in the future, I had hoped.

My most precious creation yet occurred then -- my son Eric. Motherhood was a joy. Albeit sleep deprived, I would walk the Boulevard with the stroller and ate whatever I wanted, like whole belly fried clams and true Ipswich onion rings. After our son was born, my cooking bug grew larger. I made stuffed veal roasts and chocolate mouse and strolled the town, stopping at Virgilio's bakery for a loaf of the most distinguished bread of the fishermen.

Blissfully, I would roast chickens on Sundays, and often stopped by the pier to chat with the fishermen, who used to trade me lobster and haddock for a giant plate of pancakes, sausages and muffins. On the other hand, at home was a marital relationship that may be noteworthy only for its distance and destructive posturing. Denial of serious discord was possible by diverting my energies to that beloved child in the high chair, covered with homemade applesauce. Dinner parties were also my thing to avoid the anger and fear. I made glorious eight course Chinese dinners where we ate on floor pillows or lavishly entertained with French pates or ridiculous amounts of Italian platters. I had even won a local clam chowder contest, so one season friends would gather to watch Celtics games and scoop up bowls of chowda and pans of red pepper corn bread and warm apple crisp.

How many times has that little voice in your head screamed trust your gut, do NOT do this, you do NOT want this? While hearing this message loud and clear, an overpowering meddling Mother-in-Law insisted we open another much larger restaurant. It had been a year since I had Eric and she explained to me that her son needed this. A terrible location, a room with challenges and already one restaurant that failed in the location. That was what she was hawking. I just wanted a little Cape style house with a lawn for a dog and play space for Eric. But, my little voice in my head was not strong enough to fight the will of Pat and Bud Williams and their "support" of their son. Forget it that there was a child that needed play time or a staff that needed consistent support. To put it mildly, I was stuck.

BJ's in the Park (Bill and Judi's) opened with raves about the food and our ringer server and pie maker Martha Graham. I worked very hard with a huge kitchen, (too big) and lines of 300 plus people out the door for Saturday and Sunday Brunch.

There were the nine varieties of homemade muffins and apple crisp, just like the old days, and stuffed Anadama French toast (a Gloucester specialty). Soon, the creative side realized a 4-night a week steakhouse concept would add cash flow. So, 4 nights a week we closed for an hour or two in the afternoon and hung café curtains and changed over to table cloths and menus printed on brown paper shopping bags (creative yes; but ridiculously expensive).

As you have read in previous chapters, the demise of BJ's ('bank account(s) disappearance') and the sudden death of my sister, Hilary, devastated me for some time. But, I was also given the opportunity to fight back, to rise up, and to demonstrate those skills that were sown years previously.

Baking oatmeal cookies at 4 am and pulling double shifts on the bar at a local restaurant takes backbone; this, I inherited..

There was a man who often came into my restaurants. The one that ate well done meat who I refused to date because of that very fact. He changed to medium rare, and kindly immersed himself into Eric's life (even spent many mornings following garbage trucks as my son aspired to be a trash collector).

Paul Gallagher is the fine example of giving pure love and support to a child. He helped create a more balanced life for my son. He introduced me to Sarasota, after I shared with him we could not be serious as I needed to move to a warm climate. Apparently, his thoughts exactly, as he spent so many winters traveling throughout the Florida Spring Training map, sitting in the bleachers, writing short stories.

I loved Sarasota and after five years of visiting each March, sobbing as we crossed the old rickety Ringling Bridge one last time in route to the airport. I threw out the ultimatum: after near 80 inches of snow that winter, I was moving, with or without him.

SPAGHETTI CARBONARA STYLE WITH PEAS AND MUSHROOMS

Description

I was schooled by a viewer who reminded me that true carbonara is pasta and egg yolk and cheese. True, but this dish was a crowd pleaser at both restaurants and is about as comforting as you can get on a cold night.

Ingredients

1 Tbsp. extra-virgin olive oil
2 large garlic cloves, lightly crushed
1 cup sliced button mushrooms
1/2 sweet onion, diced
2-3 Tbsp. butter
6 ounces pancetta, sliced 1/3 inch thick
and cut into 1-inch matchsticks
3/4 cup heavy cream
3 large egg yolks

1/3 cup freshly grated Parmesan cheese, plus more for serving
Kosher salt
3/4 cup fresh or thawed frozen baby peas
3/4 lb. spaghetti
Freshly ground pepper
1 cup frozen peas, partially unthawed but not cooked separately.

Directions

Bring a large pot of water to a boil.
Add salt and oil to the pot of boiling water then add pasta when rolling boil reappears.
Cook until al dente Drain well.
Note:
You want to make sure the last minute of cooking the pasta is in the sauce with cream and butter.
In a large, deep skillet, heat the oil. Add the garlic and cook over moderate heat translucent. About 3-4 minutes. Do not brown.
Remove garlic and set aside for another dish.

Add the pancetta to the skillet and cook over moderately high heat, stirring occasionally, until golden and crisp and the fat has been rendered, about 5 minutes.

Using a slotted spoon, transfer the pancetta to a bowl.

Pour off all but 2 Tbsp. of the fat from the skillet.

Add onions and mushroom and 1 Tbsp. butter and sauté until just tender. You may need to drain off some liquid if the mushrooms become too watery.

Add the cream gently grabbing the brown bits on the bottom of the pan.

Remove from heat.

Add cream and whisk in the egg yolks and 1/3 cup of the Parmesan cheese.

Heat very gently and serve with extra Parmesan cheese.

ITALIAN FISH STEW

Description

Eric began eating shellfish by age two. Clams, mussels and lobsters were abundant and his desire for fresh seafood seemed endless. Often a recipe we served at both restaurants, this is the classic of flavors and seasoning.

Ingredients

3 Tbsp. olive oil
1 large fennel bulb, thinly sliced & diced
1 Onion, chopped
3 large shallots, chopped
2 tsp. salt
4 large garlic cloves, finely chopped
1 tsp. dried crushed red pepper flakes
1/4 cup tomato paste
2 15-oz cans diced tomatoes in juice (with Italian seasonings)
1 1/2 cups Dry white wine
5 cups fish stock
1 Bay leaf
1 lb. clams, scrubbed
1/2 lb. mussels, scrubbed, debearded
1 lb. uncooked large shrimp, peeled and deveined
1 1/2 assorted firm-fleshed fish fillets, cut into 2-inch chunks
1 lb. bay scallops
2 cups cubed red potatoes, washed skin on

Directions

Heat the oil in a very large pot over medium heat.

Add the fennel, onion, shallots, and salt sauté until the onion is translucent, about 8 minutes. Add the garlic and red pepper flakes, and sauté for 2 minutes.

Stir in the tomato paste. Add tomatoes with their juices, wine, fish stock and bay leaf. Cover and bring to a simmer. Reduce the heat to medium-low.

Add red potatoes 20 minutes before finishing. Cover and simmer until the flavors blend, about 30 minutes.

Add the clams and mussels to the cooking liquid. Cover and cook until the clams and mussels begin to open, about 5 minutes.

Add the shrimp, scallops and fish. Simmer gently until the fish and shrimp are just cooked through, and the clams are completely open, stirring gently, about 5 minutes longer (discard any clams and mussels that do not open). Remove bay leaf. Season the soup, to taste, with more salt, fresh ground black pepper and red pepper flakes.

Ladle into bowls and serve with garlic bread.

SUNDAY AFTERNOON WHOLE ROASTED CHICKEN

Ingredients

1 whole roasting chicken
2 lemons
Fresh rosemary sprigs
Fresh thyme sprigs
3 Tbsp. truffle butter
Truffle salt
Garlic salt
Poultry seasoning (I prefer Bells)
2 leeks, tops discarded, washed well

Directions

Season cavity of chicken well.

Stuff Loosely with cut lemons and leeks.

Season chicken on all sides.

Brush with soft truffle butter.

Preheat oven to 350 degrees °F.

Place Chicken upside down on roasting rack in pan and roast 1/2 hour upside down. (This lets all the juices flow to the breasts.)

Turn right side up and continue to roast to 165 degrees °F.

SWEET POTATO WAFFLES WITH SLICED BRISKET AND MELTED FONTINA CHEESE

Description

    While I use leftover brisket, you can substitute ham, turkey or roast beef with an assortment of your favorite cheese. This is comfort food you may want to eat in your pajamas while watching your favorite Netflix shows.

Ingredients

Bruce's Sweet potato pancake mix
Waffle iron (I make a double batch)
2 eggs
Vegetable oil (see directions, 2 Tbsp. per cup of mix)
Water (see directions)
Whisk batter and heat waffle iron. Spray
with PAM and cook waffles.
Sliced brisket

Heat any au jus in separate pot
For topping Whisk together:
2 cups sour cream
1/2 bunch fresh cilantro
Splash cilantro dressing or cilantro oil
Minced chives or scallions
Sliced fontina cheese or asiago (two slices per waffle)

Directions

    Preheat broiler.
Place 2 cooked waffles on a pan or oven proof pan.
Dip leftover brisket in au jus then shake extra liquid off so the waffle does not get soggy.
Top with sliced fontina or asiago cheese.
Place under broiler until cheese is brown and bubbly.
Top with sour cream and cilantro sauce.
Serve with gravy or au jus on the side for dipping.
Extra waffles can be frozen and toasted when needed.

NEW ENGLAND CLAM CHOWDER

Description

I happily made this clam chowder for years at both restaurants. We "chowda" folk take it seriously. Since moving to Florida I am not always able to find the fresh clams. If you are making a large pot you can go to a buying club like BJ's and buy restaurant size cans of clam juice and clams. My ratio is 2 cans clam juice to one can chopped clams.

Ingredients

24 medium-size quahog clams, usually rated "top neck" or "cherrystone," rinsed
2 cups clam juice
1/2 lb. slab bacon or salt pork, diced
2 large onions, minced
3 large Yukon Gold or Chef potatoes, cubed
3 sprigs thyme - remove from stem (2 tsp. dried thyme also works well)

1 bay leaf
2 cups half and half
Freshly ground black pepper to taste
Sea salt to taste
Roux:
2 Tbsp. unsalted butter
2 Tbsp. All purpose flour

Directions

Put the clams in a large, heavy Dutch oven, add about 4 cups water, then set over medium-high heat.
Cover, and cook until clams have opened, approximately 10 to 15 minutes. (Clams that fail to open after 15 to 20 minutes should be discarded.)
Strain clam broth through a sieve lined with cheese cloth to remove any extra sand and set aside.
Remove clams from shells.
Rinse out the pot and return it to the stove.
Add bacon or salt pork, and cook, until bits have crisped, and fat is rendered.
Make the roux in a separate pot, melt butter, add flour and heat to medium-low, whisking occasionally.
Use a slotted spoon to remove pork from fat and set aside.
Add the onions to the fat, and cook, stirring frequently, until they are translucent and soft but not brown, about 8 minutes.
Add the diced potatoes and clam juice and simmer Add the thyme and the bay leaf.
Partly cover the pot, and simmer gently until potatoes are tender, approximately 10 to 15 minutes.
Meanwhile, chop the clams into medium size pieces (note - I also add 2 cups canned or flash frozen chopped clams).
When potatoes are tender, add the half and half and stir in chopped clams and reserved bacon.
Gently whisk in the roux, checking constancy every 5 minutes. Continue to whisk to avoid clumps
Add fresh ground sea salt and fresh ground black pepper to taste.
Let the base come to a simmer and remove from heat.
Be careful not to boil or the base will burn.
Remove the bay leaf, and discard.
The chowder is best if it sits overnight.
Cooking Tip:
If the chowder seems to thick you can add extra clam broth.
Reheat on a very low simmer before serving. Do not let the base burn or cream curdle from the heat.
Serve with oyster crackers.

SWEET POTATOES AU GRATIN

Description

Perfect alongside that Sunday Prime rib, grilled pork chops or roasted chicken, this is a comfort side dish.

Ingredients

1 cup milk
1 pt. (2 cups) heavy cream
1/4 tsp. ground nutmeg
1/4 tsp. ground cinnamon
1 tsp. salt
1/4 tsp. ground black pepper
3 lbs. sweet potatoes (about 12 sweet potatoes, depending on size), peeled and sliced thin with a mandolin

1 Tbsp. chopped fresh parsley leaves
Gratin:
2 Tbsp. butter, cut into chunks, plus more for baking dish
1/4 cup panko bread crumbs
1/4 cup grated Cheddar

Directions

In a large saucepan combine milk, cream, nutmeg, cinnamon, salt, and pepper. Gently fold in sweet potatoes. Bring to a simmer and allow sauce to thicken.

Preheat oven to 350 degrees °F.

Butter a 3-quart baking dish. Combine the bread crumbs, butter and Cheddar to make the gratin topping. Transfer the potato mixture to the baking dish and sprinkle with the gratin topping.

Bake until the potatoes are cooked through, about 35 to 45 minutes.

Serve in the baking dish, garnished with chopped parsley.

PUMPKIN CHEESECAKE WITH GINGERSNAP CRUST

Description

Just Desserts offered six varieties of cheesecakes, but to this day, pumpkin remains my favorite.

Ingredients

Gingersnap Crust:
1 1/4 cups gingersnap cookie crumbs (plus whole gingersnaps for garnish)
1/4 cup Unbleached All-Purpose Flour
1/4 to 1/2 tsp. ground ginger
2 Tbsp. brown sugar
1/4 cup unsalted butter, melted

Filling:
3 (8-oz.) packages cream cheese, at room temperature
1 3/4 cups sugar
1 tsp. cinnamon
1/2 tsp. ground ginger
1/4 tsp. nutmeg
1/8 tsp. ground cloves

1/4 cup flour
1 tsp. vanilla
1 cup pumpkin puree (not pumpkin pie filling mix)
5 large eggs
1/2 cup sour cream

Directions

Preheat the oven to 350 degrees °F. Lightly grease a 10" round springform pan.

For the crust: Combine all the ingredients, other than whole gingersnap garnish) in the bowl of a food processor and pulse until evenly mixed. Press into the bottom of the springform pan, and at least 1" up the sides of the pan. Bake for 10 to 15 minutes, just until you can smell the gingersnaps.

Remove the crust from the oven, and reduce the oven temperature to 300 degrees °F.

For the filling: Place the cream cheese in the bowl of your mixer. Blend on low speed for a few minutes, until no more lumps remain.

Add the sugar, flour and spices and mix for an additional 2 to 3 minutes. Be sure to stop the mixer at least twice to scrape down the sides and bottom of the bowl.

Add the vanilla and pumpkin and mix to combine. Add the eggs one at time, mixing well after each egg is added.

Stir in the sour cream by hand. Pour the mixture into the prepared pan/crust and bake for 50 to 60 minutes.

The cake is ready when the center 2" of the cake is still a bit wobbly. The temperature measured 1" from the side of the cake will read 170 degrees °F. Turn off the oven, prop open the door, and allow the cake to slowly cool in the oven for one hour.

Remove the cake from the oven and chill, lightly covered for 4 to 8 hours before serving.

ITALIAN STYLE BABY BACK RIBS

Description

This is the quintessential put it all in the pot recipe. Since Baby Back Ribs were on sale, I bought extra and cut the racks into halves. This way we can have BBQ ribs next weekend. (Warning! Sauce may drip down your chin! BUT it's worth it!)

Ingredients

1 rack Baby Back Ribs, cut into individual ribs
1 cup chopped pepperoni or dried salami
2 cups fresh plum tomatoes cut into quarters
6 cloves garlic diced
3 long hot peppers sliced, seeds and stem removed
3 Cubano peppers, remove stems and
seeds. Cut into large strips
2 onions, peeled and quartered
2 jars favorite tomato sauce or 2 26oz.
Pomi strained tomatoes
Pinch crushed red pepper

Vegetable oil for searing ribs
Garlic salt to taste
3 zucchini cut into chunks
Pasta (I prefer the wide noodles to sop
up the "gravy" of this dish)
Bold red wine, about 1/2 to 1 cup

Suggested Need Items:
A large Dutch oven, Le Creuset is my favorite
since you will be browning the ribs then
simmering them in the same pot.

Directions

Season ribs with garlic salt and fresh ground pepper.
Heat pan with about 3 Tbsp. vegetable oil.
Sear individual ribs in batches so you don't crowd the pot. Remove and set aside.
Add onions and garlic and pepperoni and sauté. Add a little olive oil if needed. Deglaze pan with red wine.
Add peppers and ribs, tomatoes and tomato sauce. Simmer for 1 hour stirring several times.
Add zucchini, crushed red pepper and simmer 20 minutes
Serve ribs with sauce and veggies over pasta and crusty bread to sop up every drop.

SPIRAL BEET AND GOAT CHEESE SALAD WITH BLOOD ORANGE DRESSING

Description

There was always a joke with my Mom that every big holiday she forgot to put out the pickled beets. Trust me, you won't forget to serve this dish made fresh and bright.

One of my favorite tools is the spiralizer. Keeping in all the nutrients with raw spirals of vegetables, it also makes a beautiful presentation as well.

Ingredients

4 large Beets, peeled and spiralized*
1/4 Cup Pistachios, chopped

4 oz. goat cheese, crumbled
2 Tbsp. flat leaf parsley

Dressing:
1/2 shallot minced
Juice of one blood orange
1 Tbsp. White Balsamic Vinegar

1 tsp. Honey
Kosher Salt and fresh ground black Pepper, to taste
2 Tbsp. Extra-Virgin Olive Oil

Directions

Place the spiralized beets in a large bowl.
In a small mason jar, combine the orange juice, vinegar, honey, salt, pepper, and olive oil. Shake until well combined.
Pour the dressing over the beet noodles.
Add in the parsley, goat cheese and pistachios and toss well.
Serve immediately.
I lay a double row of paper towels down under the spiralizer as we all have learned that beets stain.

STEAMED CLAMS WITH PANCETTA AND TOASTED BLUE CHEESE GARLIC BREAD

Description

As a former New Englander nothing says summer eating more than steamers, (aka steamed clams). Traditionally we just use a little water, chopped onion and the freshest clams. Add red potatoes and corn on the cob and of course a dish of blueberry ice cream for dessert and we feel that dark long cold winter blues melting away.

Ingredients

2 packs steamer clams
1 pack chopped pancetta, browned crisp
1 onion chopped
4 sprigs fresh thyme
1 cup water
2 bottles IPA beer
Fresh chopped flat leaf parsley for garnish
Fresh fennel fond (save the bulb for
an Orange Fennel Salad)

2 ears fresh corn on the cob broken into halves
6 red potatoes quartered
2 leeks, whites only washed well and chopped
1 loaf baguette
1 stick Irish or French butter
2 cloves garlic mashed
1 cup blue cheese crumbled

Directions

For the Garlic Bread:
Slice bread into halves & then quarters.
Brush with soft butter and garlic.
Broil until lightly browned.
Add crumbled blue cheese just until melted.
In a large size pot add water, 1 bottle of IPA beer and one chopped onion. Bring to a boil.
Add very well rinsed clams and cover lowering heat slightly until clams open, about 6 minutes.
Drain setting aside the liquid.
Top clams with crispy pancetta and serve with a bowl of broth to rinse out any sand particles and dip garlic cheese bread into the broth.
Garnish with chopped parsley and serve with a cold IPA.
A simple bowl of fresh blueberry ice cream or peach cobbler makes the perfect dessert with this dish.
Note:
Never store clams in plastic. Keep in netting and place over shaved ice if using the next day and store in refrigerator but I prefer always to use fresh the same day.

PUMPKIN CRANBERRY SPICE BAKED DONUTS (AND CAKE OR BREAD)

Description

The whole studio fills with the Aroma of New England spices whenever I bring out this recipe.

Ingredients

For the cake donuts:

1 stick unsalted butter
2 cups all-purpose flour (plus dusting for pans)
1 tsp. baking soda
1 tsp. baking powder
3/4 tsp. kosher salt
2 tsp. ginger
2 tsp. cinnamon

1/2 tsp. ground allspice
1 tsp. pure vanilla extract
1 1/2 cups light brown sugar
1/4 cup grapeseed oil
2 large eggs
1 (15-oz.) can organic pumpkin pie filling
1 cup whole cranberries

Frosting:

1/2 cup cream cheese soft but cool
1/2 cup butter slightly softened
1 1/2 cups confectioners' sugar
1 Tbsp. Molasses

1 tsp. fresh lemon juice
1/2 tsp. pure vanilla extract
Pinch kosher salt

Directions

Heat oven to 350 degrees °F.
Butter and flour round cake donut pans or 9 x 13 inch pan, or loaf pans.
In medium bowl whisk flour, baking powder, baking soda and spices until well combined.
Combine light brown sugar.
Butter and grapeseed oil.
Beat until light and fluffy.
Add one egg at a time and vanilla extract and pumpkin pie filling.
Scrape down sides of bowl.
Slowly add the flour mixture then fold in whole cranberries.
Pour batter into prepared pans. Depending on which pans you are using you will bake 16-25 minutes.
Frosting:
Whip cream cheese and butter.
Slowly add confectioners' sugar and then molasses, lemon juice, vanilla and pinch of salt.
Frost donuts/cake when cooled.

Chapter Five

THE JOURNEY SOUTH

The entanglement of darkness and cold gloomy skies for 6 plus months out of the year had taken its toll. My life had turned, for the better. That brown sugar and butter investment paid off. It was time to sell <u>Just Desserts</u> and begin anew, and now with a supportive husband and the most incredible Dad to our son Eric.

Gloucester, MA. was still filled with ugly memories; the warmth of our annual pilgrimage to white sands and sunshine demanded a push toward a new beginning. The sunshine seemingly always beckoned me and the glistening aqua waters pronounced that the time was now. So, shortly after our marriage, which, by the way, it snowed in the Berkshires that day, May 12th. preparations were underway to relocate south.

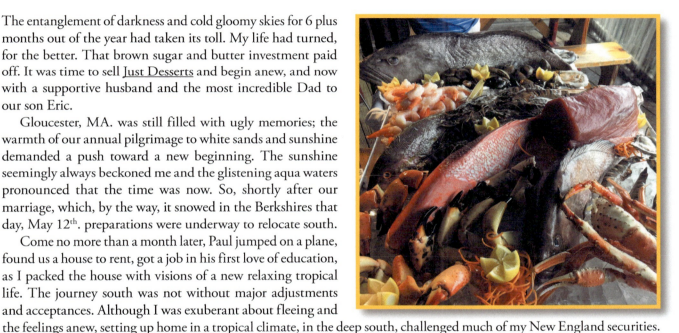

Come no more than a month later, Paul jumped on a plane, found us a house to rent, got a job in his first love of education, as I packed the house with visions of a new relaxing tropical life. The journey south was not without major adjustments and acceptances. Although I was exuberant about fleeing and the feelings anew, setting up home in a tropical climate, in the deep south, challenged much of my New England securities.

Note to all those wanting to live in a tropical climate. Do not move in August, if at all possible. The atmosphere of enormous humidity and sweltering heat will deflate your energy, let alone make you not want to cook anything other than a salad or shrimp cocktail.

There was much to learn about Florida's West Coast.

1. There is no good Chinese or Jewish Deli.
2. The only great veggies in the summer are from cooler places like the Michigan and Pennsylvania farmlands. One reverses the cooking palate. Florida strawberries start appearing in late December and Feb brings the plump roma tomatoes.
3. Grouper is the Florida version of New England's haddock and one must discover great grouper sandwiches, always searching for the freshest.
4. Sadly the beach has a tendency to become a distant cousin, though you swore it would be otherwise.

5. However, there is no better place to heal the soul, savor a Bumble Bee tuna sandwich with Cape Cod potato chips, and, watch a sunset in mid week than the beach.

For some absurd reason I gave away almost all my pots and pans, knives and 4 food processors and various other appliances. A clean break I thought. Maybe take the first year in Florida to settle my family. Now, why, I wondered as I unpacked boxes of cookbooks and serving utensils, did I give up my kitchen items that I would so desperately need? Lord only knows I received the wrong memo.

Change your furniture when you go south; not years of the pans that still wore dents and scraped edges of a long restaurant career. Memo noted to those that love to cook, bake and sauté. This is your best connection to the real you. Save them, savor them, and you can commence a new culinary chapter, with kindred memories in tow.

Nonetheless, I learned that restocking a kitchen can be most therapeutic. Simple variations -- a change from how you used to organize seasonings, or a decision to go with more wooden bowls than ceramic. Uncovered and discovered was the greatest connection to my heritage: my sister's recipe box, secrets distinctively maintained. Ironically, Hilary seldom cooked, but the recipe collection was further manifestation of her poetic self...and her ever presence. Gratefully, recipe cards of my Mom's were also in attendance. Meant to be: if I were going to be far away from Riva Cooper, her daughter was going to make the applesauce spice cake on Rosh Hashanah, as well as the Jordan Marsh Blueberry muffins that she held in such supernal regard. The Sarasota kindness, no doubt culled from the sensibilities of the large midwesterner migration, casts about a genuine friendliness. Stress, therefore, slid to the background. And, although I missed the diversity and facility of Connecticut, the 'maybe later' pace of the South was the reprieve I craved.

I envisioned plans of Mom's visits to Sarasota where I could prepare new types of fish, like grouper and red snapper. Maybe I'd also audition my first attempts at what a true key lime pie should really be. I never, however, envisioned the call I would receive just 2 months after our move south: my Mother had terminal bone cancer. Swiftly, I flew back to Connecticut and packed what few things could be gathered quickly. We moved her to our new home, where comfort and love would extend her life from 2 months to a full year.

No parent should ever survive a child and the loss of Hilary crushed my mother's will. She staggered and grieved, but also stalwartly held on. Mom needed assurance that both Eric and I had a good new life; one filled with love with someone that could look out for us and care for us.

In retrospect, this next long road proved most transformational for me. I reached deep into the inner strength and unconditional compassion that my mother (and her mother before her) had meticulously sewn into the fiber of my bones. Consuming myself with ceaseless care for a woman who daily demonstrated a kindness for all, an unswerving devotion to her children, and a grace of presence everywhere she walked was a gift. To heal her from the demons of her marriage was a wish come true.

My Mother Riva was a woman of comfort in the kitchen. Simple tastes were her favorite. Our annual egg salad sandwiches and fried red tomatoes, dutifully prepared and enjoyed on the biggest holiday of the year (The Academy Awards), remain. Simple, definitive favorites graced her meals in the tropical sunlight: mushroom barley soup, a rare roast beef, a simple baked potato.

When the horrible metallic tastes from chemo invaded, pots of fresh applesauce, gluttonous coffee milkshakes, and, an occasional bite of an adored, breaded veal chop.

The mother-daughter meals became something else - with feelings of some surreal and mystical ballet, snuggled in laughter and gentle touches. I would wheel my Mother into the kitchen and, with a full heart, observe her gently and carefully manipulate her little glass chopper for the celery.

I recall Mom once reacting in horror, as she witnessed me use bare hands for the eggs going into the salad. "Mom", I explained, "you just saw me wash my hands. It's OK! Do you REALLY want to know what happens in a restaurant kitchen?"

We giggled non-stop and hugged unabashedly. I remember feeling such deep, deep affection for this priceless moment. This innocent, graceful, and giving woman was feeling both earth's safety for a rare time, as well as accepting her inevitable encounter with death.

Just short of a year later, my mother passed peacefully in our home. She was able to let go; the cancer invaded much too quickly. But, she has never left. The aura of love and sweetness, with grin-granting memories of her skill in being able to eat 3 Fritos then closing the bag, her child-like love of sweet and sour cabbage rolls and even the occasional McDonalds hamburger and fries (shared with her new son in law) would always remain. It does, to this day.

I began to work part time again, hoping to learn the pulse of my new town. In some absurd way, I actually felt strength from the loss of my Mother. Ophelia's by the Bay proved to be the curative location. There, with pristine views, a highly competent and loyal staff, a caring cadre of guests and an exciting, fine-dining menu, I had the good fortunate to exhibit my hospitality leadership skills. The frequent visits by frolicking dolphins, emotion packed rainbows, and, breathtaking sunsets made my re-entry into the workforce one of deliberation and reflection.

Sarasota is one of the most supportive cities for women, and soon I was writing for two local magazines (with the help of some great editors). Communication about the culinary world does not come haltingly for me. Be it fermented, pickled, barbecued, rotisseried and/or sprinkled with truffle salt, dialogue around foods is healing, revealing, and engaging. Fortunately our beautiful city, with its transcendent possibilities, makes for an intriguing culinary culture.

Welcoming me into this elegance and refinement were such masters of the hospitality stage as Lee Roy Selmon, Don Guercio, Marsha Fottler, Roy Yamaguchi, and Sean Murphy. Discussions around unserving accommodation and free flowing generosity, and their place in the culinary world, were abundant with these visionaries. And, for every 'Florida Red Potato Tour' (Walmart's) that I had to endure, I was rewarded by invitations to James Beard Dinners in NYC or lodging at elegant Sonoma/Napa Estates, while visiting the Julia Child Museum, Professionally, I further found myself humbled, yet grounded, by Board positions on University of South Florida's launching of a well-conceived School of Hospitality, and, Girl's Inc., efforts to develop awareness of the nurturing capabilities of food for these impressionable and oh so precious young girls.

Before long, I accepted culinary assignments to the Caribbean, to Canada and in between. I was able to review restaurants in Rome, Florence, Venice, and Siena. And together with similar visits to Dublin, Paris, Tel Aviv, Amsterdam, London, and Brugge, I was further awoken to cuisine's innate celebration of diversity and the wholesomeness it delivers.

On a suggestion from the grand dames of philanthropy and grit, Marjorie North and Margaret Wise, I was asked to do a cooking demo and charity luncheon for about 250 people. With baskets of ingredients and cooking- burners burning, I got up on a mini stage and just began to cook...sharing my life stories….while finishing the sauces with precision and accuracy. A few local chefs also prepared foods, as I proudly served as MC.

Suddenly, and I must say to this day, shockingly, Jan McCann, a top salesperson at a small local TV station approached me. In an assertive, prolonged manner, she insisted that I was to accept my destiny to take over their cooking segments. Television…? No way, I thought. After all, I had been in the audience of the Ranger Andy Show as a child, thus fulfilling my TV career. Fate would have a different outcome for me. For at about the same time, local TV station owner and all around good-guy, the handsome Don Guercio was convincing me to start a weekly restaurant talk show. In a matter of a few weeks, I evolved from charity host chef to TV and restaurant critic chef: the Chef Judi brand was born. (One of my greatest regrets is my Mother never got to share the pride of witnessing my television career path.)

To say I was pretty bad at my audition for the cooking show is a gross understatement. I was flat, boring and stiff. But with perseverance and passion…..and studying Julia Child and Jacques Pepin for every teaching point, I started to grow this new persona. People stopped me on the street and asked for cooking tips. People called my home phone when their Alfredo Sauce broke; restaurants kept inviting me to dine; culinary segments were filmed; other artists' interviews were held. A new world, with familiar terrain, was unfolding. I tasted and chopped, chatted and swirled wine with the experts from California to NYC. Hilariously, someone saw talent somewhere on that stage performance and, with a little help from supportive friends I glided into the role and have loved every single minute of this reclaimed self.

About 5 years into the work with the two locally-owned TV stations, ABC7 called me. Over grilled steaks and a very good bottle of red wine, John Scalzi, our daytime meteorologist (an all around incredible person, while also being a damn good grill master), and I conversed about unleashing potential and my joining ABC. In a very short time, Station Manager Kay Mathers (another resilient role model) was introducing me as ABC7's Culinary Director.

The work of television is my strong suit. Unless you are nationally syndicated, television work demands a blue collar attitude: creating menus, food shopping, prepping, schlepping, cleaning up (endlessly). And this, I love! To be able to earn my due, scrub my space, show my worth, and work as one are the insides of TV. My on air persona is the sharing of that joy with others.

I love every single moment. Any day that someone stops me and shares enjoyment of the cooking shows or patronizes a restaurant or event based on my recommendation, I am so happy. That connection feels so intimate, so real. It is what it means to be human! I am as gratified as serving a perfectly executed Dover Sole meuniere with caramelized leeks and orange butter roasted spears of asparagus.

I love my world of teaching people about simple but newer and fresher versions of classics. I love my world of touching people, who just want to share the gift and goodness of food.

GRILLED ASPARAGUS SALAD

Ingredients

1 lb. fresh asparagus trimmed
2 oz. prosciutto cut julienne
1/8 tsp. crushed red pepper
2-4 quail eggs
Juice of two lemons
1 Tbsp. white balsamic vinegar
Kosher salt
Fresh ground black pepper
Pinch crushed red pepper
Cooking spray
2 tsp. extra-virgin olive oil

Directions

Heat a grill pan over high heat.
Gently break asparagus spears where they naturally break.
Discard ends.
Coat pan and asparagus with cooking spray.
Add asparagus to pan; cook 7 minutes or until charred, turning occasionally.
Place asparagus on a plate.
Add prosciutto to pan and crisp.
Set aside.
Remove pan from heat and spray with food spray.
Crack quail eggs and cook sunny side up.
Place sunny side eggs over asparagus.
Mix lemon juice, white balsamic and Olive oil, crushed red pepper, salt and pepper to taste.
Drizzle over asparagus salad and top with crispy prosciutto.
Serve immediately.
Note:
For a vegetarian option delete prosciutto and top with shaved parmesan.

MOROCCAN CHICKEN

Ingredients

2 Tbsp. purchased harissa
2 Tbsp. fresh lemon juice
2 Tbsp. ground cumin
1 1/2 Tbsp. ground coriander
1 Tbsp. paprika
1 Tbsp. olive oil
2 Tbsp. caraway seeds
2 tsp. salt
1 1-inch piece peeled fresh ginger
4 garlic cloves, peeled
1/2 tsp. saffron threads
2 3-lb. whole chickens, cut in half, backbones removed
1/4 cup (1/2 stick) butter
3 cups minced onions
1 can chickpeas, drained and rinsed.
Approximately 2 cups water
1/4 cup chopped fresh cilantro
1 cup chopped dried apricots

Directions

Stir caraway seeds in heavy small skillet over medium heat until fragrant, about 1 minute. Transfer to processor. Add next 10 ingredients. Purée until coarse paste forms. Cool before rubbing paste all over chicken halves. Place in refrigerator for up to 4 hours. When you are ready to begin cooking, remove chicken from refrigerator.

Melt butter in large pot over medium heat. Add onions; sauté until beginning to soften, about 5 minutes. Add chicken halves to pot. Add enough water to almost cover chicken. Bring to boil. Reduce heat; cover and simmer until chicken is tender, turning once, about 45 minutes. Add chickpeas and simmer 10 more minutes to absorb the sauce

Transfer chicken, skin side up, to baking sheet. Add cilantro and dried apricots to liquid in pot. Boil until reduced to 2 cups, about 20 minutes. Season with salt. Meanwhile, preheat broiler. Broil chicken until golden brown, about 6 minutes. Transfer chicken to platter. Serve with braising liquid.

PANCAKES WITH MACADAMIA NUT SAUCE

Description

On holiday mornings my job was to make a creative breakfast. This recipe comes from Hawaii, (where I indulged with Roy Yamaguchi).

Ingredients

1 cup macadamia nuts
1 Tbsp. butter
2 Tbsp. flour
1 cup whole milk
cup cream
3 Tbsp. sugar

tsp. kosher salt
2" vanilla beans, sliced lengthwise and seeds scraped out – or 2 tsp. vanilla extract
3/4 tsp. lemon juice
6 fresh bananas- preferably overripe, mashed

Directions

Pancake Mix (follow instruction and ingredients to serve four - make pancakes separately from this next recipe)
Process the macadamia nuts in a food processor until finely ground.
Spoon the nuts into a medium saucepan and fry over medium high heat for 5 minutes or until fragrant.
Lower heat to medium and add the butter, stirring until melted.
Stir in flour and cook 1 minute.
Slowly pour in milk and cream, constantly whisking the whole time.
Scrape the seeds out of both vanilla pod halves.
Add sugar, salt, vanilla seeds, and vanilla pod to the pan.
Cook 5 minutes or until thickened, stirring constantly.
Stir in lemon juice.
Pour sauce through a fine strainer into a serving dish.
Serve warm.
Serve over ice cream or banana pancakes.

PASTA WITH YELLOW PEPPER SAUCE AND GRILLED SHRIMP

Description

We ate a lot of pasta during the lean years after BJ's in the Park. Now, however we can enjoy the fruits of our hard work with fresh Florida shrimp.

Ingredients

1 (16 oz.) package linguine pasta
2 Tbsp. butter
1 1/2 Tbsp. olive oil
1/2 cup chopped red bell pepper
1/2 cup chopped yellow bell pepper
1 Tbsp finely minced garlic
48 large shrimp - peeled, deveined, tails removed, rinsed and dried with a paper towel
1/2 cup dry white wine (such as Chardonnay)
1 tsp. lemon juice
1/4 cup clam juice
1 Tbsp. butter

1 1/2 Tbsp. olive oil
1 cup heavy cream
Pinched crushed red pepper flakes to taste
3 Tbsp. chopped fresh parsley
Kosher salt to taste
2 Tbsp. finely chopped shallots
1 1/2-inch sprig fresh rosemary or 1/2 tsp. dried
1 Tbsp. flour
1/2 tsp. vinegar, preferably balsamic or malt vinegar
Freshly ground pepper to taste
EVOO

Directions

Bring large pot salted water to a boil. Add spaghetti and cook as directed until al dente.

Drain reserving 1/2 cup pasta water.

Roast and peel the peppers, Cut the peppers into cubes and set aside.

Put 1 Tbsp. of the butter in a saucepan and add the shallots, garlic, rosemary and wine. Bring to a boil and cook down by half.

Add the cream and bring to a boil. Cook, stirring often with a wire whisk, about 10 minutes.

Blend the flour with the remaining 1/2 Tbsp. butter. Add to the sauce, stirring with a whisk.

Put the pepper cubes into the container of a food processor or, preferably, an electric blender. Blend as thoroughly as possible. Scrape the puree into the sauce and cook about 5 minutes, stirring often. Add the vinegar, salt and pepper. It is not essential but, ideally, the sauce should be put through a fine sieve, preferably the sort called a chinois.

Season shrimp with Kosher salt and fresh ground pepper.

Heat large sauté pan to medium high.

Sear shrimp about 1 1/2- 2 minutes per side until pink but do NOT overcook.

Remove shrimp and add about a Tbsp. olive oil to pan.

Toss in pasta and pepper puree and wine sauce together until pasta is coated.

Garnish with rosemary sprig.

STILTON-STUFFED BAKED PEARS

Ingredients

1/2 cup packed brown sugar
2 Tbsp. butter, softened
1/2 cup crumbled Stilton
1/4 cup dried cranberries
1/4 cup chopped pecans

8 peeled Bartlett pears (about 3 and 3/4 lbs.)
1/4 cup apple juice
1 Tbsp. port
Creme fraiche

Directions

Preheat oven to 375 degrees °F.

Combine brown sugar and softened butter in a small bowl and stir until well-blended.

Add crumbled cheese, dried cranberries and toasted pecans; stir well.

Cut 1 inch off each stem end of each pair; reserve top.

Remove core from stem end and scoop out about 2 Tbsp. pulp from each pair to form a cup, using a melon baller or spoon.

If necessary, cut about 1/4 inch from the base of each pair so it will sit flat.

Place the pears into a 13 x 9-inch baking dish.

Fill each pair with about 2 Tbsp. sugar mixture and replace the top on each.

Combine juice and port in a small bowl; pour into baking dish.

Bake pears at 375 degrees °F for 30 minutes or until tender.

Serve warm.

STUFFED SHELLS WITH SMOKED SALMON AND LOBSTER SAUCE

Description

Have you noticed the trend at grocery stores? More and more prepared food items are easily available but not always hit my high marks for seasoning. Since I love to cook, this recipe combines the fresh pasta shells with smoked salmon and ricotta cheese and spinach. No time for homemade lobster bisque? I use prepared lobster bisque as the sauce and you have saved time and money.

Ingredients

24 jumbo pasta shells
2 shallots minced
2 cups fresh washed and diced spinach
1 tsp. butter
1 8 oz. package of smoked salmon
1/2 cup diced fresh chives
16 oz. part skim ricotta cheese
pinch Old Bay seasoning

1 egg, beaten
1/2 cup mozzarella cheese, shredded
2 Tbsp. milk
1 1/2 tsp. seafood seasoning
Kosher salt and fresh ground pepper
1 cup parmesan cheese, grated
1 container lobster bisque

Directions

Cook pasta according to package.

Meanwhile, in a small skillet, add butter and minced fresh shallots. Sauté on low heat until translucent.

In a large bowl, combine smoked salmon, egg, mozzarella cheese and a pinch of seafood seasoning such as Old Bay. Chop fresh spinach and add to mixture.

Drain and rinse pasta then stuff each shell with 1 rounded Tbsp. of seafood mixture. Place in a greased 13 x 9 baking dish. Stir in Parmesan cheese.

Grease 13 x 9 inch baking dish. Place 1/2 cup prepared lobster bisque on bottom. Stuff shells and place on top of lobster bisque.Pour the remaining bisque over stuffed shells. Bake uncovered at 350 degrees °F for 30 to 35 minutes.

Serve hot with a simple arugula salad.

Optional:

Chopped steamed shrimp
1 cup mascarpone to make the dish very creamy.

TURKEY MEATLOAF SLIDERS

Description

Oh as a child how I dreaded meatloaf night. My Mom didn't exactly season to please and perhaps nothing could get me to eat meatloaf until I made one using ground turkey and topped with Sweet honey BBQ sauce. Serve cold.

Ingredients

2 large onions chopped
1 red pepper, seeds removed and chopped
1/2 green pepper, seeds removed and chopped
(optional as green peppers are stronger so depending on your liking you may omit)
1 tsp. fresh or dried thyme
2 tsp. Garlic salt
Kosher salt
1 tsp. freshly ground black pepper
2 Tbsp. Worcestershire sauce
1/4 cup chicken stock
5 lbs. ground turkey breast
1 1/2 cups dry Italian bread crumbs
3 extra-large eggs, beaten 2 dashes Tabasco or hot sauce
1 cup Sweet Honey BBQ sauce, (such as sweet Baby ray's)

Directions

Preheat oven to 325 degrees °F.

Combine the ground turkey, bread crumbs, eggs, and onions and red pepper in a large bowl.

Mix well and shape into a rectangular loaf on an ungreased sheet pan. Spread the ketchup evenly on top.

Bake for 1 1/2 hours until the internal temperature is 160 degrees °F and the meatloaf is cooked through. (A pan of hot water in the oven under the meatloaf will keep the top from cracking.)

Serve hot, at room temperature, or cold in a sandwich.

My favorite way to serve this is cold with fresh coleslaw or jicama slaw on top of the meatloaf. Serve on Hawaiian rolls. Perfect for tailgating.

SPRINGTIME SALMON CROQUETTES

Description

My mom always served salmon cakes with a poached egg on top - keeping things lighter for spring approaching, I recommend you try these just as the recipe specifies. Just a little dollop of sauce is plenty.

Ingredients

1/4 cup canola mayonnaise, divided
2 tsp. fresh lemon juice. Divided
2-3 tsp. Dijon mustard, divided
1/3 cup minced scallions
2 Tbsp. minced red pepper
Pinch garlic powder
12 oz. skinless salmon
1 large egg, beaten
1 cup Panko crumbs

1 Tbsp. canola oil
1 Tbsp. plus flat leaf parsley chopped (you may substitute cilantro if you like the flavor)
1 tsp. chopped capers
1/2 tsp. minced garlic
Pinch sea salt
Fresh ground white pepper
Hungarian paprika
Poached eggs – optional

Directions

Combine 2 Tbsp. mayonnaise 1 Tbsp. lemon juice, 1 1/2 tsp. Dijon mustard and green onions with red pepper, garlic powder, salt, salmon, egg and paprika in a food processor.

Remove from processor and add panko and toss gently.

Reseason as needed. Shape mixture into eight patties.

Heat oil in large skillet over medium high heat.

Add salmon patties and cook about 5 minutes on each side until golden brown.

Combine remaining mayonnaise with lemon juice, mustard, capers, parsley, garlic and sea salt, paprika and pepper, blend well.

Serve a dollop on each salmon cake. (Or poached eggs).

GRILLED STEAK AND HERB CREAM CHEESE FLATBREAD WITH ARUGULA SALAD AND BLISTERED TOMATOES

Description

The evolution from the traditional steak sandwich. Flatbreads are turning up on so many different restaurants. From pubs to fine dining the flatbread craze is here to stay. I find using premade flatbread crust makes entertaining a snap.

Ingredients

2 flatbreads (I recommend Stonewall)
4 cups herb cream cheese
2 cups organic yellow and red grape tomatoes cut lengthwise
Zest of 2 lemons
4 cups baby arugula
2 - 3 lbs. (I tend to go heavy on the steak per my husband's wishes) sirloin steak or leftover steak
2 fennel bulbs, sliced very thin.
Lemon Vinaigrette

(may be made ahead of time, refrigerate and shake before using)
1/4 cup red wine vinegar
2 Tbsp. Dijon mustard
1 tsp. dried oregano
1 clove garlic, minced
1/2 tsp. kosher salt
1/4 tsp. ground black pepper
1/2 cup olive oil
2 Tbsp. fresh lemon juice
Whisk or use immersion blend

Directions

For best results let steak rest at room temperature for 30 minutes. Grill steak to rare or medium rare. Let rest for 20 minutes before slicing.

Preheat oven to 375 degrees °F.

Spread sliced tomatoes on sheet pan and sprinkle with kosher salt and fresh ground pepper. Roast for about 6 to 8 minutes until they "blister".

Remove from oven and set aside.

Heat flatbread in oven until slightly crusty but do not overbake.

Cool slightly.

Spread garlic cream cheese over bread.

Slice steak and place over herb cream cheese mix.

Scatter blistered tomatoes.

In a separate bowl toss fennel with arugula and lemon dressing. Toss over flatbread pizza and add zest of lemon.

Cut into wedges and serve.

Variations:

Blue cheese instead of garlic cream cheese.

Grilled chicken and artichoke hearts, grilled shrimp, or smoked salmon instead of steak.

BUTTERNUT BISQUE WITH CRISPY BACON

Ingredients

1 large butternut squash, (about 2 lbs.)
1 lb. medium leeks
8 slices thick cut bacon
Kosher salt and fresh ground black pepper
3 cups chicken stock or broth
Splash light cream

Directions

Cut the squash in half across its width. Cut these pieces in half lengthwise.

Place the squash, cut sides down, on a rimmed baking sheet and pour 1/2 - cup water over the squash.

Roast for 50 minutes, moving the pieces around with a spatula after 30 minutes so they do not stick.

Remove the squash from the oven and set aside.

Cut the leeks into 1/2 - inch pieces and add to a 4-quart pot.

Cook over high heat, stirring constantly to release some of the fat, for about 1 minute.

Add the chopped leeks to the pot with the bacon; reduce the heat to medium and cook, stirring often, until the leeks are well-softened and beginning to color, about 10 minutes.

Scoop the squash out of the flesh from the squash shells and add it to the pot with the leeks.

Add 3 cups chicken stock and 1/2 - tsp. salt to the pot and bring to a boil.

Reduce the heat to a simmer, cover the pot, and cook for 20 minutes.

In two batches, transfer the soup to a blender.

Process until very smooth and velvety.

Add salt and freshly ground pepper to taste.

Return the soup to the pot and reheat gently before serving.

Gently add cream.

Meanwhile, in a small skillet over medium heat, cook the remaining 2 slices of bacon until crisp. Drain and discard the fat. Pat the bacon with paper towels, coarsely crumble and scatter on the soup.

Serve immediately.

WATERMELON GAZPACHO

Ingredients

1 large tomato, pureed
1/2 serrano chile
2 cups cubed fresh watermelon
1 tsp. red wine vinegar
1/4 cup extra-virgin olive oil
2 Tbsp. minced red onion
1/2 cucumber, seeded and minced
2 Tbsp. minced fresh dill, plus more for garnish
Kosher salt and freshly ground black pepper
1/4 cup crumbled feta cheese
Garnish:
Sour cream
Chopped cilantro
Tortilla or fried plantain chip

Directions

In a blender, puree the tomatoes, chile, and 1/2 of the watermelon.

Pour in the red wine vinegar and olive oil and pulse.

Add the onion, cucumber and dill and season with salt and pepper.

Puree until smooth.

Pour into chilled bowls and sprinkle with dill, feta, and remaining watermelon.

Served chilled.

Garnish with a dollop of sour cream or creme fraiche, chopped cilantro and plantain chip before serve.

Chapter Six

REAFFIRMATION

Enriching, whether it be the refinement of 'High Tea on the High Seas', <u>Crystal Cruise</u> (where I overate caviar and had to go to the ship's doctor because my ankles were swollen over with high sodium), or the grace exhibited throughout my long-weekend stay with Margrit Mondavi at the Napa guest cottage at the Mondavi Estate, or the intimate bbq chicken and apple pie back porch dinner with Marimar Torres overlooking her vineyard, or, the cultivating stroll with Salvatore Ferragamo throughout the Tuscan town that bears his image, I have been endowed with considerable prosperity. I have indelible memories and an immense appreciation for the incredible experiences of hospitality that have elevated my professional path. However, it seems that with each honorable, charitably-intended culinary assignment that I am lucky to enjoy, deeper, more reflective questions arise:

- What am I supposed to do with these experiences? What actions can result from my good fortune?
- How can the culinary enthusiasm and its passion continue to evolve in a positive way for everyone?
- Hospitality, dining, food, and all its cousins, is a healing constituent. Can establishments be profitable and simultaneously build and sustain community?

While dining as an invited guest of Italy's Treviso Region (in the town of Asolo, the namesake for the infamous Sarasota theater), I can recall marveling at the exuberance and openness of the townspeople. The bustling energy, related laughter and ongoing dialogue spelled an essence for living.

And so, I wonder:

Is this no different than the vitality witnessed on the farms of Vermont, the food halls of Vancouver BC, a sunlit, tree-blessed outside-lounge in Florida, and, the incomparable food trucks of Portland Oregon? Can sharing a meal... wherever, whenever….be the epitome of revealing a piece of one's soul? Is there any real experiential difference between gathering here at The Table Creekside, brunching by a rippling brook in Sedona, or, walking Parisian streets with fresh baguette and cheese in hand? Can you see the authenticity, the joy, the connections that culinary brings?

Many people do stop me on the street or in grocery stores to speak culinary. On many an occasion people do look up my phone number and call me with a frantic cry on Thanksgiving when the gravy 'broke'. With a care that unravels from down deep, I feel so fortunate to be able to walk them through the lumps and into a glistening gravy. The same holds true during queries about cheesecakes cracking, as well as solutions when ingredients are left behind at the store.

This is what I live for: to answer a cooking question or to tweet a recipe -- to assist, to connect, to affect. I roam farmers markets only to be able to share the qualities of local cheese stands, fishmongers, food trucks, and the like.

The fact that I happen to get paid for cooking, teaching, creating recipes, shopping, and eating incredible meals is all still shocking to me. Culinary is my mission, a vocation, a devotional enterprise. You have met my Nana and my

Mother: it is who I am...my DNA is culinary. Perhaps my <u>Sarasota Magazine</u> bio describes this identity best: "Some see a bowl of ripe Roma tomatoes, I see a bolognese sauce in 4 hours."

In hindsight, my career design was revealed progressively. Religiously observing Julia Child or Jacques Pepin on the black and white tv conjured feelings of both security and excitement. The intimacy was much like the oneness experienced with Nana or Mom. However, now the reaction held more of a mature, covetable objective. Yes, I could envision someday going to France, to dine on true roasted chicken and sole meuniere. But, it would also be as fulfilling teaching young girls how to roast a chicken at Girls Inc. The power of culinary is pretty extraordinary.

I can recall that when I was first notified that I would tour the French Culinary Institute in Manhattan and then have lunch with Jacques Pepin I absolutely melted. When I received a follow-up message that the agenda also included taping three cooking segments with him I became dazed, to say the least.

When I shared with Jacques how my Mother would have loved meeting him, he smiled and told me she was watching down on us right then. With a humble smile, and that smooth skin, in his lovely accent he then offered me the crepes we made, chuckling when he said his granddaughter made even better crepes. At the end of our time together, he spoke words that not only resonate with me today but provided me with confidence for my own career mantra:

"Stay humble, keep your phone number in the book, in case someone needs a last minute cooking tip, and, make sure you join me down at the Connecticut shore."

When I asked him how I would reach him, he laughed and said: "My dear Judi, I am in the phone book."

I have yet to make it to the Connecticut shore -- but accessibility and humility continue to be the core of my culinary career. Hopefully, you'll discover these ingredients throughout my recipes.

PAN SEARED SCALLOPS WITH BACON AND SPINACH APPLE RELISH TOPPING

Description

My Mother loved to toss bay scallops with French dressing and broil. This is a modern interpretation of enjoying jumbo diver scallops.

Ingredients

Spinach, apples and bacon are just perfect ingredients to marry sweet succulent sea scallops.
3 center cut strip pepper cured bacon
3 strips applewood smoked bacon
1 1/2 lbs. seas scallops kosher salt

Fresh ground pepper
1 cup chopped onion
6 cloves garlic
12 oz. baby spinach, cleaned well

For Apple Slaw:
4 golden apples, peeled, cored and grated
Pinch apple cider vinegar

Pinch sugar
1 tsp. warm bacon fat

Directions

Cook bacon in large cast iron pan (reserve 1-tsp. bacon fat for apple- slaw).
Coarsely chop bacon, reserving an additional 1 Tbsp. Drippings for scallops.
Pat scallops dry with a paper towel or clean dish towel. Season with sea salt and fresh ground black pepper.
Add scallops to the 1 Tbsp. bacon drippings- sear 2 to 2 1/2 minutes per side. Transfer to plate.
Reduce heat and add onions and garlic to pan. Sauté about 3 minutes stirring constantly.
Add 1/2 the spinach, sauté about 1 minute and add remaining spinach. Season with salt and pepper.
Divide spinach between 4 plates.
Sprinkle with crumbled bacon and 3-4 scallops per plate.
Mix shredded apple with warm bacon fat, apple cider and pinch of sugar (optional) toss gently and place on top of scallops.
Serve immediately.

BUTTERNUT SQUASH RAVIOLI WITH PANCETTA SAGE BROWN BUTTER

Ingredients

1 (24-oz.) package fresh cheese or
butternut squash ravioli
6 Tbsp. unsalted butter
2 medium shallots thinly sliced
16 fresh sage leaves

1/4 tsp. kosher salt
1/4 tsp. black pepper
3/4 cup (3 oz.) grated Parmesan
8 oz. diced pancetta
Garnish with a Fresh sage leaf

Directions

Cook the ravioli according to the package directions. Drain and return the ravioli to the pot.

Meanwhile, heat the butter in a large skillet over medium-low heat until it foams.

Add the shallots and cook, stirring, until golden, 1 to 2 minutes.

Add the pancetta and cook until slightly crispy.

Increase heat to medium.

Add the sage and cook until the leaves turn crisp, about 1 1/2 minutes.

Remove from heat.

Season with salt and pepper.

Add the shallot-sage butter to the pasta pot and toss gently.

Add 1/2 cup Parmesan and toss again.

Garnish with a fresh sage leaf and freshly grated parmesan.

CHAI BAKED APPLES

Description

The aroma of apples baking is such a New England scent, I love roasting fruits. Using chai teas infuses a lovely spiciness to the dessert.

Ingredients

*2 Tbsp. mint-chilla chai nilla tea leaves
1/4 cup salted caramel sugar
1/4 cup cinnamon and sugar.
8 Honeycrisp or Granny Smith apples
Homemade granola or high-quality granola

Pumpkin butter
1/2 cup water
1.75 qt. vanilla ice cream, softened.
* I order this tea online but you can use a
similar high quality spicy chai tea.

Directions

Heat water to 212 degrees °F.
Steep tea leaves for 6 minutes and strain.
Allow to cool completely.
Stir tea into softened ice cream.
Mix thoroughly and refreeze.
Mix both types of sugar in a bowl.
Core apples and hollow out leaving 1/2 inch wall in each.
Coat the inside of the apples with about 1/3 of sugar mixture and bake uncovered for 30 to 45 minutes or until soft.
Sprinkle another third of the sugar on the apples once removed from the oven.
Cool slightly.
Fill with 1 scoop of the tea-infused ice cream and top with granola and a healthy spoonful of pumpkin butter.

VEGAN CHILI

Description

While I do make sure there are some meat protein options, like pulled pork to add on top of this chili, it is the perfect recipe to use for a Meatless Monday dish, or if a few Vegan or Vegetarian friends are coming.

My secret - don't tell anyone that is a picky eater but enjoys chili. Just serve it.

Ingredients

1 Tbsp. sunflower oil
1 medium onion, diced
1 cup shredded carrots
1 jalapeño pepper, seeded and minced
3 cloves garlic minced
1/2 cup bulgur rinsed
1 cup diced butternut squash
2 Tbsp. chili powder
2 tsp. cumin
2 cans mixed chili beans rinsed and drained
1 can pinto beans
1/2 cup vegetable stock
2 cups fresh diced plum tomatoes or canned diced tomatoes
1 1/2-2 cups tomato sauce.
Kosher salt and fresh ground black pepper to taste
2 splashes hot sauce.

Directions

Heat the oil in a dutch oven or slow cooker that has browning ability.
Add onions, carrots and jalapeño and sauté, stirring often.
Once translucent add the garlic and seasonings, and chopped butternut squash and stir well.
Stir in tomatoes and sauce, broth and bulgar.
Bring to light boil then simmer, stirring occasionally for 1-1/4 hours.
Toppings:
Vegan topping use cashew yogurt or seasoned smashed sweet potatoes.
Vegetarian you can pour chili over creamy polenta.
Carnivores top with pulled pork or diced flank steak.

MUSHROOM AND LEEK PASTA

Description

Simple weeknight meal! If you haven't noticed by now, I'm a big fan of mushrooms.

Ingredients

2 Tbsp. unsalted butter
2 Tbsp. shallots, minced
2 cups sliced assorted mushrooms (I
prefer button and shitake)
2 leeks washed well and sliced (bottom half)
8 oz. fresh Pappardelle pasta 1/2 to 1 cup light cream
2 Tbsp. truffle butter
Truffle salt to taste
Fresh shaved Parmesan.
Garnish fresh chives

Directions

Bring salted water to a boil.

Meanwhile cook shallots in butter over very low heat or until tender.

Add mushrooms and leeks and sauté until leeks are tender but not overcooked.

Add light cream and reduce. (If the mushrooms add too much liquid you may have to remove some.)

Pour in a cup and drink the liquid as a delicious flavorful tea.

Cook pasta as directed or until al dente and add to cream; toss to coat.

Whisk in truffle butter or paste into pasta and remove from heat.

Season with salt and fresh ground pepper IF you are fortunate enough to have a fresh truffle you can serve with truffle shavings or fresh truffle.

Garnish with minced fresh chives.

CHILLED SOBA NOODLE SALAD

Description

I honor my Mom's tradition of serving salad most nights. Dishes like this provide a balanced meal with a little protein on top.

Ingredients

1 package soba noodles
1 tsp. sesame oil
2 Tbsp. rice wine vinegar
3 Tbsp. soy sauce
1 tsp. hot chili oil
1 Tbsp. hoisin sauce
5 Tbsp. extra-virgin olive oil
1 carrot, thinly sliced or julienned
2 cups snow peas, julienne
5 green onions, bottom 4 inches, thinly sliced

1/2 cup thinly sliced napa cabbage
1/2 red bell pepper, thinly sliced or julienned
1/2 thinly sliced yellow pepper
1/2 cup bok choy
1 cup bean sprouts
1 cup drained black beans
3 Tbsp. minced fresh cilantro leaves
Garnish
3 Tbsp. sesame seeds, toasted
4 Tbsp. unsalted peanuts

Directions

In a medium stock pot, boil water, add salt and cook noodles.
When finished, place noodles in an ice water bath to cool.
Drain and set aside.
In a medium bowl combine, sesame oil, vinegar, soy sauce, hot chili oil, hoisin and extra-virgin olive oil.
Toss thoroughly and then combine prepared vegetables and noodles.
Chill for 2 to 4 hours.
Garnish and serve chilled.
Note:
This is a perfect dish to toss in leftover grilled steak or chicken.

ERIC'S APPLE PIE

Description

A dream comes true. My son took the challenge and made the perfect apple pie at his first try. Note, I was not born with the pie making gene. Thank Goodness Eric did.

Ingredients

Pie Crust:
2 1/2 cups All-purpose flour
3 Tbsp. sugar
1/4 tsp. table salt (the night before you make the crust cube the shortening AND BUTTER and place in freezer.)

1/4 cup shortening (the night before you make the crust cube the shortening AND BUTTER and place in freezer.)
12 Tbsp. unsalted butter
1/4-1/2 cup ice water
1 Tbsp. apple pie spice
1 tsp. cinnamon

Filling:
10-12 Granny Smith Apples - peeled and cored.
*juice of one lemon
1 cup cold water
2 Tbsp. Cinnamon
3/4 cup sugar

1 tsp. ginger
1/4 cup Apple pie spice
3 Tbsp. melted butter
Dusting of flour

Directions

Pie Crust:
Sift dry ingredients.
Place all dry ingredients in food processor.
Add shortening and pulse a few times.
Add frozen butter and pulse until the dough breaks into tiny specks.
Slowly pour ice water until dough begins to form and pull away from the sides. You should still be able to see specks of butter.
Dust the countertop with flour.
Remove pie crust and knead until the dough comes together. Cut in half and wrap tightly in plastic. Chill overnight.
Filling:
Cut apples into very thin slices and add to pot of cold-water with lemon. Drain and toss the lemon.
Preheat oven to 365 degrees °F.
Butter a pie dish. Dust with flour shaking off excess.
Roll out bottom pie crust and gently lay over pie pan.

With a slotted spoon, scoop the apples, letting the excess juices drip back into the bowl. Sprinkle apples with dots of melted butter and flour.

Roll out top crust and lay over apples. Cut four slits in the top for steam to escape. Crimp sides.

Bake for 45 minutes and check to make sure the edges are not browning too much (tent with foil not covering the center).

When crust is lightly browned, and apples have baked down, remove pie from oven.

Brush with melted butter and sprinkle with extra cinnamon and sugar.

FETA WATERMELON SALAD

Description

Moving to Florida, I challenged myself to create lighter recipes, simply refreshing and contemporary.

Ingredients

1/3 cup extra-virgin olive oil
3 Tbsp. fresh lemon juice
2 tsp. kosher salt
1/2 tsp. freshly ground pepper

8 cups seedless watermelon cut into cubes
1/2 lb. feta cheese, cut into small cubes* (Do not buy crumbled feta as it loses some of its flavor).
1 small red onion, sliced

Directions

Remove feta from brine and cut into cubes.
In a large bowl, whisk the oil, lemon juice, salt, and pepper.
Add the watermelon, feta, and onion and toss gently.
Garnish with the mint and serve.

GRILLED WILD SALMON WITH MUSTARD HERB BUTTER AND BRAISED LENTILS

Description

Television opened a world to revise recipes and empower the home cook. While I am not a big legume fan, French lentils cooked properly are delicious.

Ingredients

For lentils
1 cup French green lentils
4 cups water
2 medium leeks (white and pale green parts only)
1 carrot peeled and diced
1 Tbsp. unsalted Irish or French butter
1/2 to 1 Tbsp. fresh lemon juice
For salmon

4 (6-oz.) pieces skinless salmon fillet
2 Tbsp. unsalted Irish butter
Kosher salt
Fresh ground black pepper

Directions

Mustard-herb butter:
Stir together all ingredients with 1/4 tsp. each of salt and pepper.

Cook lentils:
Bring lentils, water, and 3/4 tsp. salt to a boil in a heavy medium saucepan, then reduce heat and simmer, uncovered, until lentils are just tender, 20 to 25 minutes. Remove from heat and let stand 5 minutes. Reserve 1/2 cup cooking liquid, then drain lentils.

While lentils cook, chop leeks and wash well to remove any sand or dirt. Cook leeks and diced carrots in butter in a heavy medium skillet over medium-low heat, stirring occasionally, until softened, 6 to 8 minutes.

Add lentils with reserved cooking liquid to leeks along with 3 Tbsp. mustard-herb butter and cook, stirring, until lentils are heated through and butter is melted. Add lemon juice and salt and pepper to taste.

Remove from heat and keep warm, covered.

Pat salmon dry and season with salt, fresh ground pepper and a little drizzle of olive oil.

Heat butter in a large nonstick skillet over medium-high heat until foam subsides, then sear salmon, turning once, until golden and just cooked through, 6 to 8 minutes total.

Serve salmon, topped with remaining mustard-herb butter, over lentils.

JICAMA SLAW

Description

I use this recipe to top turkey meatloaf sliders. Light and refreshing, chilled shrimp is a nice addition for a one bowl sunset picnic meal.

Ingredients

1 large jicama, peeled then cut not Julianne matchsticks
1/2 red pepper cut into matchsticks
1/2 red onion sliced very thin
2 Tbsp. fresh squeezed lime juice
2 Tbsp. rice wine vinegar
1 handful fresh chopped cilantro
Kosher salt and fresh ground black pepper

Directions

Toss all ingredients together let rest in refrigerator up to 12 hours.

SALMON POKE

Description

This is fresh and light. A perfect appetizer served on rice crackers or in a martini glass. Simply substitute ahi tuna for another classic poke dish.

Ingredients

1 lb. very salmon, diced
1/4 cup diced yellow onions
1/4 cup chopped scallion
1 Tbsp. Hawaiian salt
1 Tbsp. crushed red chili flakes
4 Tbsp. furikake flakes or Japanese rice seasoning

2 oz. Tamari soy sauce
2 tsp. sugar
1 tsp. sesame oil
1 Tbsp. fish sauce
1 Tbsp. plum vinegar
2 Tbsp. lime juice

Directions

Combine all ingredients in a large bowl and mix lightly, making sure not to crush the cubed salmon. Place in refrigerator and allow to set for at least 25 minutes.

PUMPKIN CREAM CHEESE NAPOLEON WITH CARAMELIZED GINGER

Description

I love this recipe because it is refreshing. Try the pumpkin filling on top of golden brown cheese blintzes for a decadent Holiday Brunch dessert.

Ingredients

1 sheet puff pastry - thawed and cut into 9 pieces
Filling:
1- 10 1/2 oz. jar Pumpkin Curd (you can substitute Pumpkin butter)
8 oz. of cream cheese
8 oz. whipping cream
1 tsp. vanilla extract

1/4 cup powdered sugar plus extra for dusting
1/2 tsp. pumpkin pie spice, plus extra for garnish
1/4 cup pumpkin pie filling
1 tsp. sugar
Garnish:
Crystallized ginger
Found in most gourmet stores.

Directions

Preheat oven to 400 degrees °F.

Chill beaters and medium sized metal bowl in freezer.

Place thawed puff pastry (30-40 minutes to thaw) on floured counter top.

Cut into 9 3-inch squares.

Place on non-greased cookie sheets and bake at 400 degrees °F until brown (Approximately 12 minutes.)

Cool on wire rack.

Whip cream until almost peaked.

Add vanilla extract and powdered sugar.

Whip until peaks form.

Set aside 2 ounces of whipped cream for garnish

Whip softened cream cheese and jar of pumpkin curd with pumpkin pie spice and pumpkin filling.

Add 1 tsp. of sugar.

Lightly fold this filling into the whipped cream.

Chill for 1 hour

Carefully slice the puff pastry square in half.

Top one layer with filling (about 3 Tbsp.), and top with half of puff pastry, repeat, top with puff pastry.

Garnish with a tsp. of whipped cream, sift powdered sugar, pumpkin pie seasoning and smashed pieces of crystallized ginger over the top and plate.

Let sit for 4-6 hours in the refrigerator, uncovered.

QUINOA TABBOULEH WITH MARINATED BONELESS CHICKEN THIGHS

Description

As a food critic, I am constantly battling the weight gain. Eating healthy protein bowls helps me stay healthy in between decadent meals.

Ingredients

1 cup quinoa
Kosher salt and freshly ground black pepper
1/4 cup freshly squeezed lemon juice (2 lemons)
1/4 cup good olive oil
1 cup thinly sliced scallions, white
and green parts (5 scallions)
1 cup chopped fresh mint leaves (2 bunches)
1 cup chopped fresh flat-leaf parsley
1 English cucumber, unpeeled and medium-diced
2 cups cherry tomatoes, halved through the stem
2 cups medium-diced feta (8 oz.)

2 tsp. zest of lemon
1/2 cup golden raisins
For the Chicken Thighs:
2 lbs. Boneless Chicken Thighs
1 cup No Oil Dressing (I prefer A Moroccan blend)
Garlic salt
Moroccan seasoning mix

Directions

Make day before serving!

Pour 2 cups of water into a medium saucepan and bring to a boil.

Add the quinoa and 1 tsp. of salt, lower the heat and simmer, covered, for 15 minutes, until the grains are tender and open (they'll have little curly tails).

Drain, place in a bowl and immediately add the lemon juice, olive oil and 1 to 1 1/2 tsp. of salt.

In a large bowl, combine the scallions, mint, parsley, cucumber, tomatoes, 1 to 2 tsp. of salt and 1 tsp. of pepper. Add the quinoa and mix well.

Carefully fold in the feta and adjust seasoning is needed.

Add zest and golden raisins.

Serve at room temperature or refrigerate and serve cold.

Marinate chicken thighs overnight with dressing.

Heat grill to medium high.

Season chicken breasts and grill on both sides until cooked but still juicy.

Let rest for 10 minutes, serve on top of Quinoa Tabbouleh (this dish is just as delicious the next day right out of the refrigerator for a picnic meal).

THAI COCONUT SOUP

Description

I adore Asian flavors and often host Asian themed dinner parties to get my fix of all things flavorful. My Mom used to make me egg drop soup as a child when I was under the weather, this is my version of hot Asian soup when you have the sniffles.

Ingredients

4 skinless chicken breasts bone on, cooked and shredded-discard bones
1 Tbsp. coconut oil
1 cup red onion, thinly sliced
2 garlic cloves, minced
1 Tbsp. minced fresh ginger
3 Tbsp. red curry paste
6 cups organic chicken broth
2 carrots, sliced

1/2 cup halved snow peas
1 red pepper, julienned
8 oz. soba noodles (buckwheat noodles are healthier and hearty)
14 oz. coconut milk (in a can)
2 Tbsp. of fresh lime juice
1/3 cup fresh cilantro diced
Garnish top with sliced green onions

Directions

Heat a large Dutch oven or soup pot to medium high heat. Add in coconut oil.

Once melted add red onions, sauté until translucent, about 3 to 4 minutes. Add in the garlic and ginger.

Sauté for 30 seconds, until fragrant, stirring the entire time.

Add in the red curry paste, stir the paste into the aromatics (onion, garlic and ginger) until it thickens, about 2 to 3 minutes.

Add in the chicken broth. Bring to a boil and reduce to simmer.

Add in the shredded chicken.

In the meantime bring a medium pot filled with water to a boil.

Add brown rice noodles to the pot and cook for 4 minutes (or whatever your directions say).

Remove from pot, drain water and cool the noodles with cold water to stop the cooking process.

Add noodles, carrots, red pepper and snow peas to the chicken broth pot.

Scoop about a cup of the broth out of the pot and add it to a blender or food processor, along with a can of coconut milk.

Blend until the mixture looks creamy and the broth and milk no longer separate.

Add the coconut milk mixture back to the soup pot.

Stir and simmer for 5 minutes.

Right before you're about to serve it.

Finish the soup with fresh lime juice and fresh cilantro.

LEMON RICOTTA JARS

Description

My mother was known for her lemon meringue pies. Little did I know that there was more than one way to make a lemon dessert without using her favorite "Myti fine" lemon pudding mix. My job was always to stir the pudding on the stove until the little round gelatin ball dissolved. Magic to my stirring powers and delight when I was old enough to make the meringue. This homage is a more casual dessert. Mason jars are one of my favorite food vehicles and little desserts pack nicely for a sunset beach supper or book club sugar fix.

Ingredients

4 oz. Philly cream cheese
1 jar lemon curd or one cup homemade curd.
2 cups homemade whipped cream separated
2 Tbsp. sugar
1/2 tsp. pure lemon extract
For the blueberry sauce:
1 pint blueberries
3 Tbsp. sugar
Small amount of water as needed.
1 tsp. fresh lemon zest

Directions

In a medium saucepan place blueberries, cold water and sugar.
Add zest of lemon and cook simmering until berries burst and the consistency of preserves.
Mash with a fork and Cool slightly.
Remove half the whipped cream and add softened cream cheese and lemon curd. Gently fold in until smooth.
Fill base of small low-rise mason jar with lemon cream filling.
Top with blueberry sauce, whipped cream and zest of lemon. (crumbled biscotti is a nice touch on top)
Homemade whipped cream:
Chill metal bowl and whisk at least one hour before preparing.
In a chilled bowl add heavy cream and powdered sugar to desired sweetness. I tend to keep it just lightly sweetened to let the berries and other ingredients shine.
Add 1 tsp. pure vanilla extract and whisk on high speed for about 2-3 minutes.
Check consistency often as you can over whip and cause the cream to turn into butter. On this occasion I would simply place the sweetened butter in a separate container and use as buttercream frosting for your next cake.

RASPBERRY GUAVA BARS

Description

This recipe was originally handed to me from the pastry chef at the now long-gone Colony Beach Club. Made famous by my own friends; Bambi (Famous) and Jeff Kane. I don't think I am allowed in their house without bringing a batch.

Ingredients

1/2 cup butter or margarine (at room temperature)
1 cup light brown sugar, firmly packed
1 cup All-Purpose flour
1 tsp. baking powder
3/4 cup oats (quick-cooking or old-fashioned)
1/4 cup raspberry preserves
1/4 cup guava jam

Directions

Preheat oven to 350 degrees ˚F.

Coat an 8x8-inch pan with cooking spray.

In a medium mixing bowl, beat butter and brown sugar until smooth and fluffy.

In a separate bowl, mix the flour, baking powder and oats until mixture is combined and crumbly.

Reserve 1/3 cup of the mixture for topping, and set aside.

Pat the remaining mixture into the bottom of prepared baking pan.

In a medium mixing bowl, combine raspberry and guava together until they are a smooth consistency.

Then spoon the preserve mixture on top of the oat layer, spreading as much as possible without disturbing the bottom layer.

Sprinkle reserved topping on top of preserve layer evenly.

Bake for 30 to 40 minutes or until the top is lightly browned.

Remove from oven and cool.

When completely cooled, cut into squares and enjoy!

Chapter Seven
RENEWAL OF PURPOSE

From the first time Paul showed me Siesta Key, I could breathe more deeply than ever, and, feel an overall novel sense of relaxation. There rested turquoise waters, powder white sand beaches and playful dolphins. Ophelia's on the Bay, the quaint fine dining restaurant just down the road from our beach rental reminded me of restaurants in Portland Maine and Portsmouth New Hampshire. Coincidentally, the three partners of this eloquent destination were former New Englander's. As I shared previously, the expansive dock and garden patios, offered the opportunity for respite. The lazy summer nights brought pouring rains, few customers and stunning double rainbows. The restaurant epitomized just what Sarasota meant in my life: a place for healing and renewal.

Steadily, my professional persona flourished. Having several offers of contracted work as a consultant, 'Judi Gallagher & Associates' was born. I find the excitement of teaching others as enjoyable as working the sauté pans back at Johnson and Wales. It seems whenever my hands are stirring, peeling or chopping, I am at home. A kitchen need not be defined by an industrial size. Two portable gas burners ignited, and my senses are overflowing. Answering cooking questions both live and in print place me in my habitat. My stage, no matter how large or small, is a gateway to feed people. Magic is made when a stick of butter and a cup of brown sugar become a sizzling toffee sauce, just waiting for a chance to drizzle down the sides of a New York Style Cheesecake.

It no doubt makes perfect sense that my son, Eric Williams inherited a culinary ingenuity. Even though as a youngster Eric begged me to take him for fast food and to bake frozen fish sticks and Kraft Macaroni and Cheese like the other kids' dinners, I could see his bonafide intrigue with all matters culinary. Before long, there were small hands adding extra snips of fresh herbs and an overall fascination with creations like whipping cream and powdered sugar made into soft pillows of creaminess.

Every weekend during summer and fall, mother and son would embark to Goodale Orchards, and cradle home warm apple cider donuts and an abundance of seasonal fruits and vegetables. The two of us would gather customarily in our kitchen, peeling apples, slicing vegetables, or trimming protein together, as we shared insights, dreams and laughter. In fact, for the days someone had a tummy ache, Eric learned to make scrambled eggs and cinnamon toast with my Mom. One early Saturday morning, I recall awakening to the sound of car doors shutting. Peering out a window I could see Eric, at the end of our little street, with a table, piles of toast (well gone cold) and a container of orange juice. He was charging 25 cents for the toast and juice combo or a dime for just toast. Business was brisk along the thriving street; sometime after an initial panic, I realized with an evolving pride that my son had inherited a precious entrenched gene... a skill for the culinary and a talent for marketing.

Eric's love for food borders on adventure. He has always been fascinated with trying obscure tastes, like marinated octopus salad and sautéed chicken livers. His culinary allure, much like mine, began in partnership with his Grammy (Ami). (To this day he still dreams of her stuffed filet of sole filled with mashed potatoes and topped with mayonnaise and ketchup.) Eric appreciates consistency and at a very young age was able to detect the difference between pure maple syrup and a fake counterpart. He, like me, demanded warm crusty bread with a bowl of seafood stew and the simple pleasures of watching cheese turn bubbly and brown under the heat of the toaster oven broiler. Our family getaways became culinary marathons, with nonstop visits to bakeries and farm stands along the way.

As I witness my son's relationship with food -- his advanced ability to create exotic sauces, blend newly compatible textures, and, accurately measure and precisely mix unique seasonings, I marvel at the culinary continuum. The intricacies aside, this generation is able to teach us that food, with all its glamour, provides the biology of balance.

My Nana taught me that food and its ceremony could be carefully crafted for sustenance; my mother demonstrated that meals, with their careful preparation, could provide periods of safety and peace. Although my relationship with food exudes kindness and connection, it seems almost prophetic that next generation (Eric) is taking the culinary to its deepest level: natural, organic, healthful and healing.

In writing this reflective book - with the pictures, in the recipes, by the recollections - I knew that I wanted people to love food as much as I do; to contemplate how food has molded us as people; to consider how we are influenced by those earliest memories of the warm baked blueberry muffins or by that Sweet-Aunt who always made the Spanish Rice casserole so special on top.

Imagine if we allowed ourselves to experience food the way the five-year-old child does -- the aromas coming from an oven, the transition of onion to caramelized magic, the taste of a fresh tomato with just a pinch of sea salt. Yet, the culinary world is perhaps at its most exciting and influential period. The interest crosses demographics, sparks council everywhere, and, ushers people into the world of imagination and adventure. There are workshops on flower box gardening and countless books on pickling the season's best - 'like Grandma'. There is increasingly more social responsibility and awareness of recycling and composting. Nutrition, farm to table, gluten-free, and, healthy eating have entered our vocabularies.

There is a lot more to learn regarding sustainability, as well as more support needed for local farmers, bread bakers, and donut makers. However, food, with all its simplicity and in all its grandeur, has provided for generation upon generation the commerce of care and comfort. It is a business that Chef Judi is most proud to be a part of!

TURKEY PAN GRAVY

Description

My mission was always to learn how to make perfect sauces. Shimmering and smooth and a gravy for Thanksgiving that was not too greasy, (sorry Mom). My Mom made a deal with me, I could attend Johnson and Wales if I learned to make the smoothest shimmering turkey gravy- no lumps.

Ingredients

Gravy Master

Directions

The key is making a roux. Melted butter and Wondra flour of equal part. Melt the butter and whisk in the flour until a thick paste.

Low heat cook, using whisk for ten minutes.

Remove all but 1/2 cup pan drippings.

Add 1 1/2 containers of turkey stock and fresh thyme and heat in roasting pan.

When the stock is a low boil slowly begin to whisk in the roux, whisking heavily to avoid lumps.

Add 1 tsp. gravy master and keep whisking until thickness is desired.

Lower heat and slowly whisk in a cup of half and half

Tips:

If the gravy gets too thick add more hot stock.

Season with poultry seasoning, salt and pepper as needed.

Printed in the United States
By Bookmasters